ATHOS

Matthew Spencer was born in Oxfordshire. He read Classics at Corpus Christi College, Oxford and took his MA in The History of Christianity, specializing in early monasticism, at King's College, London. As well as writing on religion, he reviews restaurants for *Time Out Paris*, and currently works in the IT industry.

Athos

TRAVELS ON THE HOLY MOUNTAIN

Matthew Spencer

Published in Great Britain in 2000 by
Azure
1 Marylebone Road
London NW1 4DU

British Library Cataloguing-in-Publication Data

A catalogue record for this book is available from the British Library

ISBN 1-902694-02-3

Typeset by WestKey Limited, Falmouth, Cornwall
Printed in Great Britain by Omnia Books Ltd, Glasgow

CONTENTS

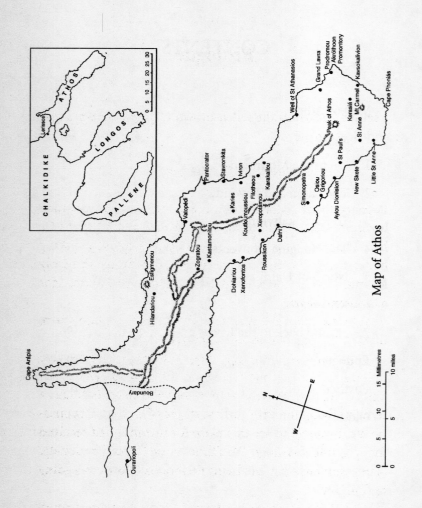

Map of Athos

Prologue

I settled back into the faded brown Olympic Airways seat and closed my eyes.

'Why are you going to Thessalonika?'

I opened them again to meet the gaze of a young Greek man beside me. He was heading home from London, where he had been studying music. And so, for want of anything better to say, I told him. I was going to Athos, the Holy Mountain, where no woman has been permitted to tread for a thousand years.

A pause followed. And then, 'Well that's a place where most of the population will never go.'

I smiled back uncertainly. Did even Greeks feel unhappy about Athos' existence in the modern world? Since I had first mentioned to friends at college that, after a term studying the very earliest stages of Christian monastic life, I wanted to see this place for myself, I had received many gentle warnings. 'You'll be bored.' 'You'll be lonely.' 'They won't like you not being Orthodox'. Now I was going to find out.

In fact, it had not been a hard decision. Looking around for something to throw myself into after college, I found myself reading everything but the usual job-files. In the less hopeful parts of the university circular, there nestled a bizarre advertisement. Applicants 'with an interest in monastic life' were invited to apply for the post of guest-house-keeper at the Lavra monastery on Athos.

Rushing to the library I found everything I needed to know about Athos, and the Grand Lavra itself. If I was going to dip my toe in the waters of modern religious life, I was choosing an interesting strategy. Not only is the Holy Mountain a single-sex paradise – or prison, depending on your view – but the monastery of the Lavra is the oldest and most venerable of all Athonite convents. I had the chance to go straight to the heart of Athos' version of that intriguing experiment in holiness, common to so many cultures: the ascetic life.

Phillip Schofield, the young Byzantine scholar who had placed the advert, was sanguine. Since he had survived a stay of some days, he was full of encouragement that I should see this most beautiful part of northern Greece. Who after all has had a chance to spoil it? But that is another story.

*

Athos is part of the Chalkidike peninsula that hangs down from Macedonia in the northern Aegean. One of three promontories, the Holy Mountain, known in pre-Christian times as Akte, reaches out into the sea some thirty miles, and is at no point more than about four miles wide. Within this territory, Greek law exists alongside a unique arrangement. The Mountain's religious prohibition against women, and even female domestic animals, was thus – though it remains to be seen for how long – enshrined in the secular Greek constitution.

At the end of the same long finger of land rises the huge majestic peak of Mount Athos itself. Beloved of Zeus, and hallowed from ancient times – even as emperors have presumed to hack at its base – the Mountain remains the immovable symbol of eastern Orthodox spirituality. For the Orthodox, as for others, Athos points heavenward, a vision of holiness, according to a way of life that started almost spontaneously in the early Church, and which has been part of Christianity ever since.

Getting to the Mountain is not easy, even in these ecumenical times. I was warned at some length in the very first letter I received from an Athonite monk, that I would need to come with a panoply of documents. In addition to letters of recommendation from worthy persons – an Orthodox bishop was suggested – there was also the matter of a consular letter, obtainable only *in situ* at Thessalonika. The steps were clearly described, and yet I could not help thinking they were a formidable barrier across which to arrive at the fabled hospitality of the hermits and monks who occupy the Mountain.

Time was when this band was getting ever smaller by the year. The Russian monastery alone had several thousand monks during the nineteenth century. Then came the great falling off, from which Athos has finally begun to recover. Now vocations are up, although tensions are as great as ever between the manifold forms of ascetic life which Athos, like the rest of the monastic tradition, has always known. For myself, I was not going to judge. How could I, knowing so little about the reality of ascetic life? In fact, despite being a convert to a tradition which values these things highly, I had journeyed a thousand miles to step inside my first monastery.

I knew there were big questions about such places, and about Athos in particular. Quite apart from the obvious one, the subject of more than one newspaper article each year –

why are there no women? – the presence of dedicated celibate communities on Athos, closed off from the rest of the world, asks us to consider directly the Christian view of life far more than do most political arrangements inside the European Union. But what exactly is it that Athos is saying? To what, if anything, does the whole strange structure bear witness? Does it have anything at all to do with the rest of us, whether we are religious or not? Such questions, and others, arose as I made my way on foot around the peninsula. It is these that I found myself trying to bring into focus, not necessarily to come up with answers, but in order that I might better learn what the ascetic life asks of us, and what we in our turn must ask of it.

On Athos, I had cause to think often of Phillip Schofield, the Byzantine research student whose advert in *The Bridge*, and a subsequent meeting in my college room, prompted me to set out for Athos in the first place. I hope he may not now entirely disapprove. Theoliptos of the Lavra was a fine host, as I knew from Phillip's words he would be. Yet I know he would not mind me saying that a whole set of people have guided this book. This includes a number of friends, family and teachers, as well as Christopher Palmer and the Trustees of the Palmer Scholarship for whom I first wrote the story of my visit to Athos. Above all, it includes those whose simpleness of heart, much more than any learning or official wisdom, has made them examples of holiness on Mount Athos. To them and to all those men and women who have tried to connect the ascetic life with those people living in the world, I owe this book. And so, in the words of one Monk Theoliptos, 'Well to come to Athos!'

I went through to the other side of the stone walls . . . I felt guilty. I was here out of curiosity, a spiritual voyeur, an ecclesiastical window-peeper. What's more such cloistered spirituality made me suspicious. Dubious about men who sought changelessness to release them from uncertainty and turmoil, I questioned a faith that has to be protected by illusory immutability. Intimidated by ignorance of Trappist beliefs, I was uneasy about what I imagined went on in a monastery . . .

Monasteries, I knew, were remnants from the Dark Ages – dying vestiges of medievalism – and monks were religious atavisms. Why would a sane man sequester himself? Renounce the world? How could he serve a religion that makes so much of love among peoples and then keep to himself?

> William Least Heat Moon (William Trogdon),
> *Blue Highways: A Journey Into America*
> (New York: Fawcett Crest, 1984).

CHAPTER 1

On to the Mountain

*The monks of Athos rise before the sun and go to sleep
before it sets. They follow a calendar and a way of life
the rest of the world has forgotten and which must at
times seem misguided, even to them. Into the world of
the Mountain, foreigners have strayed for many reasons.
Some have come to leave the world – that other world
which Athos has pledged to forget. Others have come to
learn – of its life and its treasures: the priceless books
and art that remain after so much has been stolen from
the Mountain through the centuries. Still others have
come to gawp, a not ignoble tradition perhaps, and one
that has produced some intriguing insights into the life
which is still lived, a millennium after its birth, on the
Holy Mountain of Athos.*

On Sunday, 1 August 1993, I flew to Thessalonika –
ancient Salonica – capital of the modern Greek prov-
ince of Thrace and Macedonia, and one of the very last centres of Byzantine life to fall to the Turks in the fifteenth
century. As the all-important northern capital, guarding
vital trade routes, Thessalonika had been bolstered by a huge
set of walls, rivalling those of Constantinople itself. Culture
kept pace with fortification and Thessalonika has been left
the proud possessor of one of the greatest collections of

Byzantine churches in the world. When it finally fell to Sultan Murad II in 1430, the axe of the Turkish threat was lifted high over the head of the Holy Mountain. Five hundred years of monastic life must surely now be crushed by barbarian greed. And yet, incredibly, when the smoke cleared, Murad took the opportunity of his decisive hegemony in the region to recognize and safeguard the autonomy of Athos. The cradle of Byzantine Christianity, defender of the faith through years of heterodoxy in the imperial capital, was now to be under the protection of the Ottoman.

The Turks were those most effective of conquerors, absorbing and assimilating where their heritage was outclassed. As with the Church of the Holy Wisdom at Constantinople, they recognized a unique, if alien, cultural wonder. While *Agia Sophia* became a mosque, the ecclesiastical polity of Athos, on the other hand, was to survive without the slightest interference in government or faith. The treasure-house of Byzantine monasticism could look forward to a second half-millennium in many ways more secure than its first.

Constantinople's tutelage had always been a mixed blessing. Graced by patronage with fantastic wealth, the lost simplicity of the Mountain soon attracted the attentions of the pirate. The Byzantine empire was often slow to help, and it was in panic that the vulnerable communities took themselves to the comparative safety of their high towers, as they waited for the imperial fleet to arrive. Now with occupation, Athos seemed paradoxically to escape molestation. Its new, militarily effective masters had a better grip on the region than the old empire had enjoyed for hundreds of years. Beyond that, the reign of the Ottoman was surprisingly kind to Athos.

From the seventeenth century on, a *kajmakam* or adviser was appointed by the Sublime Porte. In 1912, when Turkish control ended, the departing functionary summed up his case for two French travellers.

> Look around you, look at these thousands of monks; visit their monasteries, question them yourself. Of what, in reality, can they complain? Have we touched their rules? Have we violated their property? Have we forbidden pilgrimages? Have we altered a single item of their secular organisation? . . . Always the West is talking of Turkish fanaticism. But what race, I ask you, what conqueror could have treated these people with greater humanity, greater moderation, greater religious tolerance? Under our law, they have remained as free, even freer than under the Byzantine Emperor. And . . . they have not had to endure under our domination a hundredth part of the vexations that you have imposed on your monks in France . . . They will regret us, Monsieur.
>
> from Michael Choukas, *Black Angels of Athos*

Since Turkish control ended, the political fortunes of Athos have been tame by comparison. Other challenges, however, may be in the pipeline. Certainly the most important event of the twentieth century was the decision of modern Greece to grant the peninsula the status of 'semi-autonomous republic' within the wider state. According to this settlement the Sacred Community of Athos regulates travel to and from its territory and levies its own taxes. Under the watchful eye of a Civil Governor appointed by Athens, it even makes its own laws, including those concerning the more bizarre aspects of monastic rule, such as the exclusion of women, female domestic animals, and beardless youths. These conventions for the most part date back to the first few hundred years after the Holy Mountain was founded as a monastic colony, in about the eighth century of our era, and they have to do with the ascetic principles behind the life that is lived there. (Some of them are considerably older even than a place as ancient as Athos.) Yet the modern world is not easily kept at bay. There is already talk of making the region subject to European law on equal opportunities. When that happens it will be an interesting time for the debate on asceticism's place in the modern world.

The territory of the Holy Mountain is not easy to get to, or to remain in, even if you are a man. In fact it has never been. When Robert Curzon, redoubtable pilferer of artefacts from luckless monasteries throughout the Levant, sought entry in the early nineteenth century, he had to attend, in order to obtain his permit, a meeting of the Epistasia, the executive of the monastic government of Athos. This four-man conclave remains to this day at the head of an unchanged political structure. Every year each of the twenty 'ruling' convents elects its representative to serve on the Council at the capital, Karies. The representatives are divided into five groups of four, and each of these groups takes it in turn to form the Epistasia, which governs the peninsula from the imposing assembly building in Karies. Under the constitution established in 1924 and ratified two years later, all the Holy Mountain's land is parcelled out in separate territories to the 'ruling' monasteries.

At the same time, there are many other communities of ascetics living on Athos, and many hermits following their chosen way to God in isolation. Each of these sets of monks, both the anchorites of the Holy Mountain and all those monks who live under other types of monastic arrangement (the so-called semi-eremitic kinds of community, for example) are, strictly speaking, under the control of the twenty main convents. Within each of their separate territories, you will find village-like groups of dwellings, known as 'sketes' (*skitai* in Greek) and also homesteads – with two, three, or slightly more monks in them – known as *kalyvai*. Smallest of all are the so-called cells, the *kellia*, lonely outposts consisting in the main of a single monk, often perched on the most inaccessible ledges of a cliff-face, or else deep in some wood.

In all this, the secular state impinges to a remarkably slight degree. Greece sends an ambassador to Karies as well as a division of police to enforce, where appropriate, republican law. On the ecclesiastical side, the Ecumenical Patriarch of Constantinople reserves the right of jurisdiction which has been exercised by his forebears to great unpopularity over the centuries. It was, nevertheless, with secular bureaucracy that I had first to make contact to gain my *diamonitirion* or 'monastery pass'.

*

The Kafkaesque corridors leading through the Ministry of Macedonia and Thrace to Room 218 are trodden each day by hordes of Byzantinophile foreigners. Ten non-Orthodox are admitted each morning, and may stay normally for no longer than four days. By brief interrogation one Mrs Plessas, at that time, established the worthiness of one's motives. One should have a genuine interest in Byzantine art or monasticism or the like, although it sometimes proves sufficient to be a 'man of letters'! The ministry would be most impressed by an introduction from the Patriarch of Constantinople such as Curzon was able to unpack from his mule in the 1840s. Failing that, however, the obtaining of a letter of recommendation from the British Consul makes for an atmospherically Graham Greene-like diversion. At 11 am on Monday 2 August, I placed mine on Mrs Plessas' desk. It read:

> The British Consulate present their compliments to the Ministry of Macedonia and Thrace and have the honour to request them as to be so good as to grant a permit to visit Mount Athos to the undermentioned British subject.
>
> The British Consulate avail themselves of this opportunity to renew to the Ministry of Macedonia and Thrace the assurance of their highest consideration.
>
> George C. Doucas, Honorary British Consul

Once I reached his monastery, Theoliptos explained that I might be able to secure the necessary privileges, from the Epistasia, for a longer stay. In the first place, I had to make it as far as Athos itself. So the next morning, after a three-hour journey from Thessalonika as hair-raising as most bus trips in Greece, I was deposited at the one-boat port of Ouranopoli with the rest of my band of hopefuls – some foreign, mostly Greek, with many fathers and sons, spanning an enormous range of ages. Here the additional trial of the 'Pilgrim Bureau' – in reality a trestle-table, behind which sit three officials of surly aspect – detained me for a further hour. At this point no amount of permits, recommendations or reassuring consular letters will deter its 'staff' from declining to issue you with a *diamonitirion* if they don't like the look of you. One hapless western priest was turned back on account of the 'Reverend' title in his passport. When he returned from Athens with altered documentation, he realized he had forgotten to change the photograph showing him in his dog-collar! In the event, he bargained his way through, converted to become a monk and has stayed ever since – a worryingly common phenomenon.

The bus had been thick with Orthodox clerics in stovepipe hats. At the port the concentration increased still further, thronging the quay with priests and monks in black garb of varying degrees of unkemptness and putrescence. (This is very definitely no insult in the monastic canon.) There was no increase of politeness. I had to fight my way on to the pilgrim boat which lay at anchor dwarfed on all sides by the huge sightseeing vessels which ply around the coast, offering to the uncommitted and the unpermitted an all-too-brief glimpse of the convents and hermitages that line the shores of the Holy Mountain.

From Ouranopoli the pilgrim boat rounded the first blunt promontory of the southern seaboard, to take us beyond the border between secular and sacred Athos – now impassable via the landward path. Gradually sections of the line of monasteries that stretches from here to the port of Dafni came into view. Zografou and Kastamonitou are screened from the shore by the dense woodland that wonderfully still covers the vast majority of the peninsula. But from Dohiariou onwards, at each coastal convent, the boat bears round to collect those pilgrims too infirm, exhausted or indolent to progress on foot.

Dohiariou is a beautiful walled garden in which orange and fig trees guide you up the slope that rises uniquely within the enclosure. Next come Xenofontos and Agiou Panteleimonos, bleaker in their dishevelment. The latter, especially, is a decaying monument which testifies to the

Russian hegemony on Athos during the nineteenth century. Rife weeds spill through the burnt-down and deserted out-buildings – rows of barracks built for the thousands of monks who once filled the place. Last along this coast comes Xeropotamou, hidden high above the shore, on a plateau. In time I would visit all these, but first came Dafni and an appointment with my host, Theoliptos.

As the boat pulled in, the jetty bustled with pilgrims, clerical and lay, waiting to return to the mainland. A clapped-out bus crawled round the corner to head back to Karies from where it had brought exiting pilgrims for the return sailing: fare and timetable stipulated by the Epistasia, since there is no transport deregulation here. Indeed all con-nections revolve rigidly around this single arrival and departure of the pilgrim-boat at 11.45 am each day. A small *kaiki*, or launch, continues along the south coast and up the north-eastern side of the peninsula as far as the Lavra, ferry-ing the weary and the unfit. The whole three-hour journey costs about a pound.

None of this concerned me now, however, since I was met by an exuberant Theoliptos, urgently shaking my hand and protesting the impossibility of carrying 'so many monks' back to the Lavra in his jeep, a most modern and smart con-veyance, of essential four-wheel drive but somewhat otiose nattiness. The complacent frowns of my fellow Lavra-bound pilgrims seemed strongly to suggest that it was I, and not any of the monks, who would be duly left behind.

Theoliptos continued to frantically importune his charges. What to do with me? Would I perhaps like to stay one night at the local *skiti*, and continue up to the Lavra the next morning, accompanied 'on ze mu-les' by the taciturn non-Anglophone monk standing at his side? I acquiesced to this picturesque proposal, rather liking the idea of arriving at my host's monastery like Robert Curzon, on the back of a beast of burden. But it was not to be. In true Athonite style arrangements evaporated on a whim and somehow the entire complement, hoary and young, were bundled into the back of Theoliptos' all-terrain monk-mobile.

We climbed steeply up and away from Dafni on a dirt road built between the port and the capital for the millennial celebrations in 1963. Since then further thoroughfares have been carved, worryingly for the conservation-minded, across swathes of the Athonite wilderness, which remains so marvellously, for the most part, intact. The best map of the Holy Mountain is published by Reinhold Zwerger and Klaus Schöpfleuthner, two Austrian devotees who return every year to update their cartography. As the network of tractor-trails spreads, visitors plaintively consult their Zwergers of former years to find that yet another scar has been drawn across the beautiful face of Athos.

*

At a later stop on my journey, I had a long conversation with a young Cypriot novice, a *dochimos*, about the pace of development and progress on the Mountain. Athos, he felt, had held out a long time – the first chainsaw and gas-cylinder arrived in the mid-1960s – but since the first incursions, the slippery slope of technological advance and dependency had fallen sharply away. Much of what I ate in each community was home-grown – vegetables and fruit including tomatoes and watermelons. On my last day at the Lavra I would find myself in a giant circle of monks and pilgrims, all of us weeping our eyes out as we peeled baskets and baskets of onions. Where did these come from? I wondered. Minutes later I was guided to a storehouse for my next job. Here the

floor stretched for yards; half of it was covered with the tou-
sled fruits of the onion-harvest. My detachment had to strip
the lot for the remaining peelers. The other half was a carpet
of potatoes! All this produce, however, is the fruit of the
most modern farming methods – fertilizers are deployed in
abundance. My companion, Dimitrios, lamented the ecological treason this comprised. 'If we can't even look after a
lump of earth, how can we look after our souls?'

Interestingly, there is a parallel to this in the architectural
curacy of the monks. Everywhere I went on Athos, new
building work was carrying on apace – hardly a monastery
without spanking new guestquarters built from the best
cedar and pine the mountain affords. The style of construction produced remarkably pleasing new wings looking like
nothing so much as a page from an Ideal Home catalogue.
But what price modern western tastes, cry the purists, in the
cradle of Byzantine monasticism?

And yet, after my time on the Holy Mountain, I came to
feel strongly about the issues involved here. First, it was ever
thus. My guidebook protested at the 'hideous nineteenth
century exonarthex next to the katholikon', the main church,
at the Lavra. However, the monasteries of Athos are first and
foremost thriving and vigorous religious communities, and
in no way the mere custodians of fossilized Byzantine
theme-villages. Aged buildings are ruthlessly gutted or
replaced wholesale, as they have to be. A German architect I
met remarked how insubstantial Greek buildings generally
are, being built to last a couple of hundred years at the most,
and for summer, not winter, occupation – a major reason for
my visiting Athos when I did. Each monastery, excepting the
solider features of churches and fortification towers, must
have been rebuilt or replaced in entirety over the years.

Perhaps problems arise when functional concern meets historic or artistic importance and eager monks do not stop to consider their debt to the architectural heritage in their custody. Yet the cavalier appearance of their treatment is, I suggest, paradoxically a very part of the often untutored vigour which has caused that heritage to survive. The monks treat their surroundings as their home and furnish them accordingly and in the light of their modern tastes and needs. Thus an extension to the church in the nineteenth century brought aesthetic incongruity just as enlargement or renovation of *archondariki* (guestquarters) brings it today. In both cases the functioning of the institution in question remains justifiably paramount.

A second factor is undoubtedly the background of those coming to Athos as monks today. Whereas in the past, novices would have been raised from early youth in the cultural environment of the Holy Mountain, now the majority come to it as a change of direction, via conversion from the sterilities of the secular life which many feel has failed them. They bring with them, therefore, their experience of life in the world and the skills they learnt in it. Perhaps throughout the centuries such a pattern of cross-fertilization always existed. Certainly today the artificial generation that sustains the monasteries on Athos continually imports the culture of the world beyond — a culture from which self-propagating communities, like the American Amish, tend to be far more insulated.

And yet 'traditional' Athos seems unlikely to be submerged. Monastic life depends heavily, for example, on the motor vehicle, but equally common is the sight of a lone, aged monk struggling uphill on his staff, or a pair of cassocked mule-drivers on missions between monasteries.

So it is hard to determine which of Theoliptos' proposed modes of arrival would have been the most authentic. If pressed (as I most certainly was by the heap of clerical luggage piling up on top of me) I would have to plump, agony as it was at times, for this ride.

*

In the course of my travels I was to hitch lifts in all manner of service vehicles. They got bigger through my sojourn till, at the height of exhaustion on my penultimate walk, I was rescued by a huge transporter and borne aloft into the heavily be-iconed cab. (Every jeep or lorry boasted a strip of adhesive icons on the dashboard or above the mirror or wherever they could be installed to assume their tutelary office.) Ritual observance on the road, as it happens, can have alarming consequences. The monastic driver of this particular vehicle had a particularly ample display – we very nearly crashed as he made the sign of the cross in passing a roadside shrine. In Greece proper these are common and highlight accident blackspots most usefully. On Athos the chain of consequence goes rather the other way!

The drive to Karies is not a scenic one. Making a dash for the capital it cuts headlong through the wooded backbone of the Mountain. The road structure on Athos has, for the most part, spared the ring of footpaths which runs round the coastal monasteries. Undoubtedly it has affected the habits of pilgrims, however, many of whom succumb to the enticement of transport between the stops of their retreat. The facility is liable to change, even wholly determine, their itinerary. Few round the southern cape, except by the *kaiki*, and this makes the trip but once a day. But much more importantly motorized transport has altered the very nature of the pilgrimage. The privations and peculiarities of Athos remain (often they are one and the same) but the physical ordeal, the way of the pilgrim itself, has become a different experience.

I am not saying no interest can remain for the traveller in the modern version of this way. In addition to the boat, after all, there is the all-too-picturesque comedy of monastic hitch-hiking: tractor-trailers bearing erect throngs of monks aloft; 1950s lorries driven hell-for-leather as you brace yourself on the open-air platform, grappling the rail behind the cab, while, from the safety of the latter, a maniac monk throws the vehicle, and his charges without, from side to side in lurches that would defy death (yours, of course, not his); and finally the spectacle of the conductor on the pilgrim-bus who counts out your change with all the surly zeal and seriousness you might expect on metropolitan transport services – even as you swerve round another train of mules at twenty miles per hour.

All this is certainly diverting, but is it the point of a retreat? The Scandinavian scholar Rene Gothoni has recently explored two different conceptions of pilgrimage that are relevant to the modern experience of a visit to Mount Athos. Orthodox pilgrims, he suggests, tend to structure their time on the Holy Mountain, around a series of stays at particular monasteries, where they would hope to talk with certain spiritual guides. Because the focus of their time on the Mountain is a set of spiritual events, rather than the process of getting there, they are more likely to hasten from one monastery to the other, using the most convenient means possible. The paradox here is that usually it is non-Orthodox westerners who tend to be more intent on pursuing a key part of the pilgrim experience, the journey itself, by classically arduous means. This leads, in turn, to the spectacle of backpackers like me struggling with large burdens just as demurely crisp-shirted, elderly Greek gentlemen, fresh from a leisurely boat-trip, are about to escort their sons and grandsons up the final approach to the next monastery on their itinerary.

The long stretch of dirt road beyond Karies to the Lavra constitutes the major injury done to the walking-paths. Swallowing what was once a rocky path, it has left a bleak procession of identical curves of sand and concrete snaking their way around each bluff. At least a consolation is afforded by the flat coastline, as you cast your eyes away from this horror and out to sea. Looking back from the road beyond Karakallou, there is the prospect of the great majestic line of convents – Iviron, Stavronikita and Pantocrator. I was to appreciate this on my final day's walk. For the moment, perched on the rear left wheel-hub of Theoliptos' jeep and craning my neck over a mountain of monks' bags – the monks at least might have walked, I mused sorely – I was unable to see much more than the trees and sea on opposite sides of the car.

The ride takes two hours, only twice as quick as on foot, and much less than half as satisfying. Still there were highlights. We stopped at a saw mill superintended outside working hours by a pair of hoary old monks, one of whom was, when I returned here on foot a fortnight later, the only swimmer I ever caught sight of, clerical or lay. The activity is considered trivial and is illegal for foreigners and punishable by expulsion. The old gentleman in question wore an old-fashioned all-in-one costume in a fetchingly ascetic shade of black. Perhaps this attire would lessen the offence in the eyes of any patrolling police, the *astinomia*, who might be on the look-out for recalcitrant natation. For the moment though,

I was the focus of attention, as Theoliptos chose to take this opportunity to test out my ingénue Greek accent. How much of the prologue to St John's Gospel could I remember?

Halfway between this mill and the Lavra there is a shrine to the Virgin Mary, the Panagia of Greek nomenclature, under whose tutelage a spring surfaces, a few yards from the path. Inside a tiny chapel, I had my first taste of Orthodox ritual. No more than two or three misericords had been squeezed along each wall and from one of these I watched my host and his assistants light a pair of lamps before the iconostasis. A box of matches lay to hand, but it is not unusual on arriving at the metal box on stilts, that is many a wayside shrine, to find a cigarette lighter lying in the bottom of a tray. Passers-by relight any dead candles and there are few more satisfying experiences than arriving at a shrine that has been recently so tended.

Beside this spring a row of stainless-steel mugs hangs on nails. In a netted larder cupboard biscuits, olives and cheese sustain the pilgrim – how often replenished, I wondered. The water was delicious, though much more so when I arrived here again on foot, three hours from Karakallou, a fortnight later. I was certainly glad to know my way to the spot then.

The steps up to the shrine were lined with pots of flowers and herbs. As we mounted them, Theoliptos bent down to run his hand through the basil. In this land of no women, it is remarkable how the apportioning of tasks differs between the two types of monastic establishment. In the great coeno-bitic convents, a life of subsistence sets the fruit of the earth on the tables of the dining hall, the *trapezaria*, with the aid of every working member of the community – and, I suppose, the prayers of the others. From onions to watermelons, the procession of tasks involved in the preparation of each food rolls on at the hands of many assistants. Pilgrims come and go; the monks themselves have different chores and studies to attend to, but somehow each day the stew gets its onion. The work is, of course, genderless. Age, fitness and the stage of one's vocation are the sole determinants.

It was a little different, however, in the smaller dwellings I visited. Here tasks, it seemed, were divided by personality type. In the skete of Kavsokalivion where I spent the first two nights of my walking tour, a place famed for its monastic artists, I lodged at the guesthouse attached to the *kiriakon*, as the main church of such a settlement is known. In a kitchen beneath my dormitory, a monk of a certain age tended the pots on the range and welcomed pilgrims with *ouzo* and *loukoumi* all the day through. By sunset, his housemate would return at the end of a day in the workshop to be greeted by the clatter of pans and plates that heralded the arrival of supper. A more worldly division of labour is hard to imagine.

I wondered at Theoliptos as he sniffed domestically at the basil. Theoliptos the rally driver, apothecary and dentist: man of dynamic talents. Perhaps only in the constantly changing duties that sustain the life of a coenobitic monastery could he find his nature fulfilled – the alternating sequence of tasks that carry life onwards here. Theoliptos, though he may like to cook with the rest of them, could not, I suspect, live in that kitchen at Kavsokalivion.

CHAPTER 2

The Lavra and Beyond

Our motley group of monks and pilgrims bumped to a stop outside the front gate of Theoliptos' monastery. The road from the shrine had been the very worst of all. Here, where the contours of the coastline are enough to snarl up the designs of the best-intentioned road-planner, our jeep had been reduced to a walking pace. Theoliptos in the front grappled the wheel round one sandy hairpin after another. Seen from the confines of this vehicle, registered on the Holy Mountain – *Agion Oros* – as AO 15, the forest at this southern tip of the Mountain seemed more ominous than any of the others I would pass through during my stay. I was glad when finally we crawled up a slope to emerge into a clearing beside the monastery itself. Theoliptos swung open the boot, releasing us from our hubcap prison. We were at the Grand Lavra.

My home for the next few weeks, and base of my travels throughout Athos, was a place of mystery, as well as tradition. Not only is it the oldest monastery on the peninsula, but the Lavra has retained its position at the top of the hierarchy constituted by the twenty 'ruling' convents. Bureaucracy aside, it is a place of great beauty. Nestling between the spurs of a coastline unchanged since the days of Byzantium, the low-slung Lavra appears less forbidding than the precipitous monasteries of Athos' southern coast.

From the outside it has the appearance of a small town. A host of buildings in differing sizes and styles jostle each other inside the walls. The threat of pirates, I was going to discover, is still engrained on the Athonite consciousness. Yet the defences at the monastery are less obvious than elsewhere. Without the natural bulwarks of a Simonopetra and the other convents of the south, in the tenth century the monks built an enormous, stocky tower at the heart of the Lavra. Its purpose? To guard treasures more than men.

Before we could go in, we had to wait. If I learnt one thing on Athos it is the difference between worldly plans and monastic ones. Travelling around other parts of Greece, I have often been struck by the phenomenon of the sudden pause. In the world of Greek transport, it is almost a convention. How many times have I sat at the back of a bus parked on some mountain slope waiting first for the driver, and eventually for all the assembled villagers, to negotiate our onward path? No matter what the obstacle – a flock of goats, a police checkpoint – the sense of absolute impasse, so strong in the first moments of quarrelling, almost always begins to evaporate on a whim. Sometimes, I have noticed, it takes a stovepipe-hatted priest for the moment to click. Which is to say that priests, or monks – who seem to do just as well – represent something of a wildcard, one needing to be played at just the right time against the general panic. Once I passed a police checkpoint with two priests in our bus. As soon as a row was bubbling with the *astinomia*, the first priest up at the front summoned his partner from the back, and all was well; we were on our way in no time.

Is the plenitude of monks the reason why the usual mediterranean phenomenon of irritation-building-to-sudden-anger is less easy to find on Athos? With endless reserves of them to draw on, who could ever cause an insoluble crisis? This may be the lay view, but it reminds me of the story from the Desert Fathers, in which two old monks try to have an argument after living in harmony for many years.

The first monk puts an object in the centre of the table between them, and tells the other to pick it up. When he does, the first monk says, 'That is mine,' to which the second replies, 'No, it is mine.' 'Very well,' says the first, 'in that case, take it and go in peace.'

Unfortunately, not all monastic disputes on the Holy Mountain have been solved quite as easily. Nevertheless the story reminds us of the peace that is the object of the monastic life: not peace as the absence of war, nor worse as war duly waged by other means. Nor beyond these, can it be the false peace of artificial isolation. Instead of all such things it is the peace that comes from seeing life differently. Thomas Merton, who lived the contemplative life for many years at a monastery in Kentucky, wrote at length about the new perspective that ascetic life can cultivate in all of us. Moving beyond our 'normal' way of doing things helps to change and even expand the way we see others. Such a change in perspective can come from lifelong dedication to the monastic way, or it can come from short periods of ascetic living, spread across the years of a normal life. In some cultures, life is broken up into different phases, so that after the period spent setting up home and family, a time of reflection ensues. As Merton saw, the wisdom which comes with such a time – a wisdom that becomes a resource for the whole community – is itself far more the point of ascetic life than the specific practices inside a monastery.

A new perspective comes from experiencing other cultures too, and so we perhaps have much to learn from Greek life, as it is lived both on and off the Mountain. On Athos itself I came across the same traits familiar from my wider travels in the country, traits that can be especially frustrating when converted into their ascetic form; for example, the habit of changing plans wholesale, as if upheaval were the normal tenor of life. And yet even here I wonder if it would do us non-Greeks good to learn a new way of relating to things. Life, after all, is seldom simply a matter of our own intentions. The awareness of this, promoted by that one particular national quirk, may fit far better the nature of reality – a reality we can control much less than we like to pretend.

Now as we waited at the gate to the Lavra, not at all in control, Theoliptos was inside transacting some business as yet unmentioned, perhaps unplanned. The pause gave me the chance to stretch my legs, and so I wandered over to the gazebo perched above the view down to the shore. This was, I remembered, the same scene that must have been enjoyed by Theoliptos' forebears down the ages, the same scene that brought one Athanasius of Trebizond, the friend of the Byzantine emperor, to found the Grand Lavra in this place a thousand years ago.

*

No one knows why Athanasius chose the spot, and yet, nestling as it does at the edge of the fabled *eremos*, the outer desert of Athonite monasticism, it must have seemed a place redolent of the utter unworldliness the saint was seeking as he and his train pushed up towards the slopes of Mount Athos itself. Hermits had lived here perhaps for as long as two centuries before Athanasius came on his imperial mission: to set up a monastic foundation to where the emperor himself might in time retire. Nikephoros Phokas never lived to see that time, for he met a bloody end at the hands of conspirators, yet his legacy has lived on far beyond most of the other secular achievements of his empire. Where else on this earth does a way of life survive that has been lived continuously in a single place, since the days of Byzantium?

With such longevity comes controversy. Hermit life was thriving on Athos before Athanasius ever arrived on the scene, and sadly the kind of monasticism brought by the Lavra has not always lived in harmony with that life. This cannot be because of conflicting goals, for throughout the eastern tradition anchoritism has coexisted with, and sometimes even within, the coenobitic way, as the form of monasticism based on a shared life in community is called. Often the elders of a monastery are those who are considered to have conquered the sin of pride, and to be ready to retire into spiritual solitude. No longer is the presence of others needed to temper their humility, but rather they can now ascend to the communion with God that is the traditional object of the monastic life.

Sometimes the elder – known as a *gerondas*, or *staretz*, in the Russian tradition – will continue to live at a short distance from his monastery, in order to be available to any of the younger monks who need his counsel. As with Father Zosima in the *Brothers Karamazov*, such a ministry can extend to those outside the convent walls.

And so we come to the nub of a great problem on Athos, a problem when Athanasius arrived, and a problem that survives to this day: How are different models of the ascetic life to live together when their paths to the same goal – communion with God and a life lived in peace with others – seem to conflict? For here on the Holy Mountain as in other places too, it is true to say that the claims of the coenobitic tradition have been taken to prove the way of the hermit is an inferior form of the true monastic life.

Where this idea comes from is hard to say. The voice most widely quoted is that of St Basil, who is frequently heralded as the champion of the common or, coenobitic, life. Yet Basil now seems to have been connected to patterns of ascetic life that have as much to do with the variant forms so contemned by coenobite critics. Certainly Basil has some harsh words to say about the dangers of the hermit life ('If you live alone whose feet will you wash?') and yet his own style of monasticism was probably less that of the regimented military-like structure of St Pachomius – many thousands of monks living in barracks, under the control of 'centurions' – than a freer semi-eremitic model, in which monks might live out their individual prayer lives, even as they nurtured a sense of communality. How loose the association between monks was in this model is a matter of debate. Yet what we do know is that Basil himself was an inspired monastic legislator, combining radical strategies for meeting the needs of the world around with a dedication to spiritual interiority. If his particular solution to the tensions between action and contemplation was as brilliant as it was unique, we should not be surprised.

On Athos, too, a form of semi-eremitic life grew up in the Middle Ages. Known as the idiorrhythmic life, it is particular to Athos, while bearing similarities to other historical models. In an idiorrhythmic convent – or skete for that matter, since both can be structured this way – the monks observe their own prayer hours and may eat on their own. At the same time communal worship is a key feature, generally taking place once a week on Sunday in the main church, known as the *kiriakon*. The model has been controversial, and is still considered a monastic experiment by some, over three hundred years after its coming to Athos!

Yet if the ruling monasteries control all sketes and hermitages in their territory, this is not to say that alternatives to the coenobitic life are wholly foreign to them. Not all the major convents, when I visited, lived according to this model, although it should be remembered that in recent years great acrimony has been caused by alleged attempts by some to impose the common life on communities who have opted to stay idiorrhythmic.

What, then, would Athanasius have had to say about all this? Apart from perhaps being a little sad, he might well have found he himself had divided loyalties. In 963 – the year when the Lavra's founding charter, its *typikon,* was granted – a general ban on the setting up of new monasteries was in force throughout the Byzantine empire. Fed up with the behaviour of existing ones, Nikephoros Phokas decided to outlaw all bequests for new foundations.

None of this was to cause a problem for Athanasius however, since Nikephoros presented him with a loophole. While creating full-scale coenobitic convents was disallowed, setting up communities of the semi-eremitic type was not. Intriguingly, for those who feel the idiorrythmic life has had a bad press in Athonite monasticism, the name of the monastic model the emperor decided to tolerate was a *lavra.*

Lavrai had been around for hundreds of years, having originated, it seems, in Syria. The name is Greek, and most likely means a 'corridor' of monastic cells, or set of dwellings arranged along a single path. This arrangement, sounding uncannily similar to idiorrhythmicism, provided both a focus of community, as well as a practical means of access between each cell. It is also, most probably, the very model of late antique monasticism favoured by Basil, the much-touted champion of coenobitic life.

All of this poses some serious problems for coenobite ideologues. Athanasius, it seems, could not have set up a coenobium, since he was expressly forbidden to do so by the laws of his friend and patron, Nikephoros Phokas. More significantly still, the monastic model he chose – presumably with the permission of the emperor himself – was that of the semi-eremitic lavra, a model with a venerable pedigree in eastern monasticism, and one that could be fairly claimed as the forerunner of idiorrhythmic developments on medieval Athos.

Yet Athanasius himself remains a shadowy character. We seem to know less about him than many monastic founders, and much less about his ideas. Was he perhaps after all a closet coenobite, forced by political circumstances to call the common-life monastery he had always longed to found on Athos, by a different name? Perhaps we shall never know.

*

Soon Theoliptos returned, to lead us through the gates of the Lavra. It was a nervous moment for me. As I stood waiting for him at the gazebo, I remembered that Theoliptos was the living representative of all that I had read and thought about, concerning the strange experiment which first captivated and then changed the Church in the fourth century of our era. Very shortly, I was to have my first experience of that experiment, as it lives on in the Church of today, the way of life known as monasticism. Waiting at the gates of my first monastery, it occurred to me how great my expectations were, both of him and the community of which I was about to become part.

In early Palestinian monasticism there was a tradition that the stranger who came to the monastery was to be considered as much a member of the community as those who lived there permanently. Passers-by, whether in need, or simply seeking rest, were to be taken in – 'received as Christ', as Benedict puts it. Only after a while, was Paul's precept, in his second letter to the Thessalonians, taken at face value: 'If anyone will not work, let him not eat.' And just as in ancient times, so it would unfold for me also. How would I fare as a member of the Grand Lavra for a season?

Theoliptos led us through the imposing portal of the monastery. Immediately inside was a shrine before which, in spite of its curious Turkish-looking inscription, pilgrims stopped on entering to do obeisance. Beyond the gatehouse, a series of heavily fortified courtyards led from one to the other, and finally into the central area of the convent. Here, among a throng of buildings that served a whole range of purposes, were several churches. As at most monasteries on Athos, the Lavra has a main one, the *katholikon*, and a number of smaller places of worship. Roundabout is an array of living quarters and workshops and then, in pride of place opposite the main church, the building that is so vitally important to the spiritual, as well as to the material, life of any monastery: the dining hall, known in Greek as a *trapezaria*.

As we emerged into the main courtyard, we were suddenly whisked off to the left up a staircase to the guesthouse, and so left behind the teeming scenes of an Athonite day in full swing: monks and mules gathering for a journey – perhaps to another convent, perhaps to one of the Lavra's own farms. Inside the guesthouse itself, the *archondarikion*, the first truly quiet moment of the day awaited, as well as a chance to get to know our host, the *archondaris*, Theoliptos. Each Athonite guesthouse, I would discover, is a law to itself. Each one would be different, in outward furnishings as in mood; Theoliptos' was to prove no exception.

Mostly, arriving from the trail, you are glad to sit down, and the softer the divan the better. Now I was glad of the hard upright chairs that were gathered around a dining table, to which our host promptly ushered us. We were all exhausted and glad to be in the cool for the first time since early that morning. And so my first Athonite welcome slowly unfolded – my first monastic one, too.

Normally, when you arrive at a monastery on the Holy Mountain, you are straightaway presented with a tray of goodies. The formula never changes, designed as it is to restore the wayfarer with an unbeatable combination: sugar, caffeine and alcohol. (These monks certainly know a thing or two.) On your tray, you will find a thimbleful, or more if you are lucky, of *metaxa* or *ouzo*. Beside it sits a cup of that wonderfully bitter coffee general to the southern mediterranean, and perilously lined with a never-to-be-disturbed sludge of grounds; while lastly, to top the whole thing off, a plate of *loukoumi*, each containing, if you are especially favoured, a single pistachio nut at its centre.

All this I would discover much later. In the meantime, Theoliptos took from his junior a large watermelon, grown, like most of the things eaten here, on the Lavra's own estate. Snatching up a knife, our *archondaris* fell to carving great slices for my fellow pilgrim and me, as well as for himself. We set about eating with gusto, and as we ate, I noticed, for the first time, the novice standing motionless at Theoliptos' side.

Novices on Athos – in Greek they are known as *dochimoi*

– have a uniform which could hardly have been foreseen by Athanasius. Since they are not yet permitted to wear monastic black, everywhere on Athos the uniform comprises a blue sweatshirt and jeans. I liked the notion that must lie behind this dress – a postulant comes in the most basic clothes he can lay his hands on. Such after all was the original purpose of monastic dress, back at the time when what monks wore was the simplest, and often thinnest, of everyday garments – not, as now, some of the most complex. Perhaps there is something to be said for modern religious being recognizable, and so maybe the Jericho Benedictines have it right. Their dress, designed to be worn casually alongside ordinary people, both connects them with those they serve, and serves to make them stand out. Their habit is much like the Athonite novice's: jeans and a denim hooded pullover – a nice balance of the modern and medieval.

The *dochimos* beside us now was doing the very job I had considered back in Oxford (working in the guesthouse) and here alongside him was my would-be employer. A monk for ten of his forty-five years, I found Theoliptos to be a man of some charisma and dynamism, an air of authority belying the relative youthfulness of his vocation. His abilities were well in evidence – not many *archondareis*, after all, can double as community dentist and rally-driver. (Is it disloyal to say, even so, I am glad not to have had toothache while on the mountain?) As a result of all his talents, Theoliptos finds himself in charge of a good many of the daily operations at the Lavra.

As I weighed up the pair, my two first real, live monks, I noticed my host's beard too set him apart from the more flocculently challenged. Reflecting an embargo not only against women but also 'barefaced youths', beards are a matter of requirement not aptitude, and so, throughout Athos, the hirsute rub shoulders with those of somewhat more minor cilial endowment. (How, I wondered, did the school which was once based in the capital Karies, get around this prescription?) In Theoliptos' case a tuck-down pony-tail, kept in typical Athonite fashion beneath his straight-sided black monastic cap, completed the picture.

When we had finished eating, we talked about how I was going to spend my time, and so I had the monastic day explained to me. The monks rise at four in the morning, western time, and begin their day with Matins. After a short break there follows a longer service – the 'Leitourgia' or Mass – after which the first meal of the day arrives around eight. Mondays, Wednesdays and Fridays are fast days, when the monks do not eat at all until the evening, although a small but tasty breakfast is served to the laypeople and guestworkers staying in the community. After the morning service, periods of work alternate with ones of rest, until the evening when there is another shorter service. After this, the monks are able to spend some time chatting with each other, or with the current crop of guests, until they retire, very early, to bed.

Not only in the east are those who come to a monastery, from the outside world, extremely important to it. St Benedict observed that the monastery is never without guests, but at the same time he encouraged discernment. His detailed rules may echo the early Palestinian tradition: after feeding guests the first few days, they are to be given work to do for the next. A stern warning is also given against those monks – the *gyrovagi*, or wanderers – who have made a profession out of receiving hospitality, and who avoid doing any work in return.

In time, I would be set to work at the Lavra. For the moment I was learning to wend my way through the vagaries of monastic dining. Nuts and honey, the early-morning fare on fast days, are one thing, but bread and olives – the staples through the rest of the week, accompanied by some tasty, albeit very oily, dishes – may be quite another for the untrained western stomach. Also, on fast days breakfast was washed down with a delicious cupful of mint tea. It was quite another story, however, on other days.

Several months before my trip, I met a priest who had visited Athos in the 1960s. 'How are you going to eat?', he asked enigmatically.

'Oh well,' I said, 'I suppose I shall be eating with the community.'

'That's what I mean,' came his ominous rejoinder.

It is true, as people warn you, that rations are not especially generous on the Mountain. Yet neither are they inadequate, even after a good day's walking – and this is despite the fact you will never, unless particularly lucky or resourceful, get to eat meat during your stay. What tends to disturb westerners rather more than the size of the portions, however, is the remarkable phenomenon of 'lunch'.

On the days when there is no fast, the morning liturgy is succeeded by a full-scale repast of oleaginous ferocity. Emerging sleepy-eyed from the *katholikon*, you will be assailed by dishes of oil-drenched ochre, lentils, peppers, rice and bowls of salad over which, for good measure, you are expected to pour a good dose of even more olive oil. On the first day this may seem unbearable. Later on it gets to be delicious. In any case, as you quickly realize, a pot of lemon-juice – rarely, I think, vinegar – is provided to protect the stomach-lining. Even more pleasingly curious at this hour, the whole thing is washed down, on feast days and Sundays, with a goblet of wine – taken after a mysterious second bell, and never before, as I was sternly reminded on my third day at the Lavra.

If you do not go to Athos with humility, you will certainly learn it there. Others I met would, in the course of their stay, find themselves upbraided for, among other things, wearing sweatpants or shorts, and for crossing their legs at meal-times – this last considered to be a sign of disrespect. The rules are at least clearly set out: they also proscribe whistling, swimming, and riding down the main street in Karies on a horse. The one thing that still confuses is the warning against long hair in a pony-tail, of which most monks necessarily fall short. Do novices grow it once they are installed on the Mountain?

Quibbles aside, mealtimes offer some of the most holy and meaningful moments in the day-to-day life of a monastery, on Mount Athos as elsewhere. At the Lavra, food is taken at a double-row of horseshoe-shaped marble tables along opposite walls of the *trapezaria*. To my mind, it cannot be an accident that so much monastic time is spent eating in company with others. In a place given over to prayer and silent contemplation, this part of the day could have been organized so differently. Yet just because it is a time when the whole community shares the same space – even though no words are said save for the readings and prayers that murmur quietly on – mealtimes are for me a part of the monastic *horarium* when people in a monastery most connect with each other: a time when you are quietly conscious of your shared humanity, even as you sit elbow to elbow, concentrating on the same actions and thoughts, helping one another to what each needs.

Benedict himself spends much time discussing the protocol at meals, as he does the other practical details of the common life; and so, while on Athos, I found myself thinking often of the Father of western monasticism. So much that passed by each day seemed to follow his prescriptions, and to have the same quiet rhythm of concern. That monks in the East and in the West share this rhythm, as they ponder the truths that all too often seem far from our world, reminds us of the power of the quiet gesture in that world.

At the start of each meal, after the customary prayers, a lector began the passage of holy reading. My Greek was not good enough to follow, but understanding in the conventional sense is a small part of the point. (In *lectio divina* – as holy reading is known in the West – you learn to read with the heart as much as the mind.) The noise at the tables gradually subsided as people drew to the close of their meals, and after the final prayers, all rose for the abbot's recess. As he and the senior monks made their way out into the courtyard, just touched by the bright Greek sun, we slowly followed, edging out of the door to congregate round the beautiful covered font, the *phiale*, which stands beside the Lavra's famous cypress tree.

Benedict is often proclaimed a master of moderation and, as I saw the same humane principles at work in the life of a modern Greek monastery, it was not hard to believe what the scholars tell us – that he must have drawn on the very same sources to which my host was a direct heir. Since guests are to be treated gently as well as patiently, I seemed to have been spared, during my first week, the worst rigours of the strange Byzantine day. Most mornings, I was woken not for the first office but for the second. It was still dark outside at this time of course, but as I stood in the gloom between narthex and sanctuary, listening to the quiet deep voices and watching the censor move slowly up and down the row of misericords, I felt how good it was to be up and awake, and praying, at these moments of the day.

Not all things on Athos however are equally kind and gentle. Take the *trapezaria* at the Lavra, for example. In general the dining halls of the Holy Mountain are amazing places, where you will often find the finest frescoes possessed by a particular monastery. The Grand Lavra itself is no exception. The most important art on Athos is divided between two fifteenth-century schools, the Cretan and the Macedonian, and it was the master of the former, one Theophanes, who decorated the Lavra's own *trapezaria*. These same paintings are the ones Robert Byron, every Byzantinist's favourite travel writer, went to research in the 1920s. Whatever the merits of his intriguing theory, on the missing link between eastern and western painting, Byron kept himself at a lofty remove from what he thought was the superstitious content of these paintings, as it had remained the superstition of his hosts' own lives.

Theophanes' huge Last Supper covers the south wall of the building, while along the side walls there is a procession of heroic martyrdoms – some of them very grisly indeed, as is particularly the Orthodox style. It is all in all a stunning scene, and the art is particularly fine. Yet more important than the execution is the drama itself, which Theophanes has been able to bring out better than most. It is important to realize that these images, in this particular place, are not cultural relics, but the very articles of a living faith. On the Holy Mountain, it is almost palpable how much the stark notions of medieval Christianity – the all-or-nothingness of the quest for heaven – have not been softened. The torments that abound in Athonite representations of hell are fully meant to be as real as they are graphic.

If we forget this, and think we are intended to be inspired to pray by the aesthetics and not by the content of all this art – beautiful as it certainly is – we miss the point of that art in its own context. It is not decoration only but a set of beliefs in graphic form, put up in spaces designed for a way of living and thinking about God, the walls of refectories as of churches.

If I needed a reminder of this, I certainly got one the next morning. After the main meal, the formidable 'lunch' was over, I offered my services to Theoliptos for any manual work he might wish me to do. (I had read just enough not to wait to be asked.) In case anyone might still be in doubt, there was the tart quotation from Hesiod over the door in the *archondarikion*: 'Work is no reproach, but laziness a great one.' Here at last was some Greek I was able, thank heavens, to understand.

Most mornings I was put on floor-washing fatigue in the company of a young Greek monk who had spent time in England. The riskiness of life in the world did not reassure Christos who seemed to be back in the days of general alarm on Athos. As we stood looking out to sea from the topmost turret, the blood drained from his face. 'In old days', he shivered, 'bad men come to kill the monks.' Clearly Christos felt safer at this height, but still he was not completely happy. 'If this was Britain,' he mused forlornly, 'they would make this place a museum.'

Was it not to be cherished though, I asked, this lack of concern for any 'heritage' market? Did the monks themselves really want to live after all in a Byzantine theme village, a kind of Athos Disney? Christos, however, was worried about preservation. He felt, as do others, that the fabric of the Holy Mountain – both natural and man-made – was under as much threat as its ancient patterns of life.

Besides, like anyone else monks appreciate diversions. Living in a place as dramatic as Mount Athos brings these in good number. Most recently there had been the visit by the cellist, Rostropovich. He came, accompanied by a minister of the Greek government, to take some monks up in his helicopter for a quick aerial tour around their home. Several days later, Athos enjoyed the faintly bizarre experience of welcoming King Constantine to the only corner of his realm still happy to receive him. As an Anglos, I was expected – however Republican my sympathies might be – to know all about this eagerly awaited event. Monks and politics have often it seems made strange, not always entirely virtuous, bedfellows.

Christos himself was a gentle man, but he had an air of shellshock about him. Was it the upheaval in his life before he made it here to the monastery in which he would probably end his days? As a young man he had travelled to London to work. Seventeen years later, in 1991, he returned to Greece and, strangely – for such choices are always strange, even to those who make them – to Athos.

Even for those of Greek origin, it is not so much the national homeland of Greece they seek in entering an Athonite convent, although all who do so must adopt Greek citizenship. Rather it is the spiritual *heimat* of the Holy Mountain itself. In any case, many of those whose families emigrated from Greece, grew up more at home in the culture of the new country, whether Australia or Britain or somewhere else. Paradoxically (since monasticism is not fundamentally about national identity), the journey to

Athos takes them right back to the heart of traditional Greek culture.

It is, as I'm suggesting, a journey to a very medieval kind of Christianity. Perhaps this is difficult to understand for those of us raised in the liberal religious atmosphere of the West. It does not take long on Athos to catch on. 'Come here, Matthaios,' beckoned Christos as we sat in the *archondarikion*, refreshing ourselves with a cup of sweet coffee after our morning chores. He pointed to an icon on the wall. 'This', he said firmly, 'is why we come here.'

The picture itself was of poor, not to say tacky, design and painted in luminous colours. It showed the procession of souls to heaven and to hell, at the Last Judgment. Heaven was cloying and hell a toothless rival beside the more terrifying portrayals of familiar western representations, or indeed next to those of the *trapezaria*. Yet it was impossible not to be impressed that here once again was theology in action, the counterpart to the spiritual education Christos was receiving every day at the hands of his teachers in the monastery.

It was not by any means entirely familiar to me. 'Matthaios, have you heard,' Christos searched his vocabulary, 'of the customs-posts?' he exclaimed delightedly. As your soul ascends to heaven, he explained, it must pass through a series of what are called in Greek *telonia*. These are staffed by demons who confront you with the memory of your sins, attempting to claim your soul, literally dragging it from the path, or ladder – as it often represented – up to paradise. 'They know everything, they have lists,' warned my companion, tapping his head.

Feeling somewhat ignorant, the next day I decided to spend a few hours reading in my cell. Sure enough, the first

book I happened to turn to – Cyril Mango's *Byzantium* – fell
open at a passage echoing Christos almost word for word:

> Life on earth was . . . lived on two levels, the visible and
> the invisible, of which the latter was by far the most
> significant. Ordinary mortals were not aware of the
> contest that was continually taking place on account
> of their salvation, but men of holiness could actually
> see and smell the spiritual beings, both good and evil.
> The final act occurred at the time of a man's death and
> shortly thereafter. For when a human being was about
> to expire, a throng of demons would hasten to his
> deathbed in the expectation of gaining possession of
> his soul and would be opposed in so doing by the
> guardian angel. Once the soul had been parted from
> the body, it had to journey through the air and stop at
> a number of 'customs-posts' or 'toll-houses' (*telonia*)
> manned by demons who examined it on its deeds and
> either let it proceed upon payment of the appropriate
> due, calculated in good works, or seized it there and
> then.

Had I read this passage first I suppose it would have been
with no more or less than the usual degree of curiosity such
things excite. Coming to it after the words of spiritual confi-
dence I had received from Christos' lips the day before, it
seemed like a great echo from the past, an echo whose source
I had heard! Encountering a living belief at firsthand, it was
impossible not to smile at its earnest historical elucidation
by an Oxford professor. Christos' own words seemed in ret-
rospect to speak as weightily as the ancient texts quoted by
Mango. According to these:

there were twenty-one 'toll houses', each representing one of the following sins: slander, abuse, envy, falsehood, wrath, pride, inane speech (including laughter, jokes, obscenity), provocative gait and licentious song, usury coupled with deceit, despondency coupled with vanity, avarice . . . drunkenness, remembrance of evil, sorcery and magic, gluttony (including prohibited eating during fasts), idolatry and heresy, homosexuality male and female, adultery, murder, theft, fornication and finally, hardness of heart.

It is to say the least an intriguing list – as much a manifesto of what Athonite life is held to be about by those in authority there (remember: no whistling or riding on horseback through Karies), as it is a reminder of how many leagues distant our own sensibilities as modern western Christians are from such precepts. Then, just as I was thinking that was the lot, even Christos' lists did not pass by unremarked:

the presiding demons were in possession of detailed ledgers (*kodikes*) in which every particular transgression was entered with its exact date and the names of witnesses. Only when a person had fully confessed a sin on earth and made expiation for it was the relevant entry erased from the ledger.

A major achievement of course of recent scholarship on late antiquity has been to reveal how far the practice of the early Church was influenced by Roman ideology. The role of the bishop – as well as that of the lone ascetic hero, it has now emerged – was to combine the functions of the Roman *patronus* regarding his clients. Bishops like Ambrose and

Augustine would remain indebted to the pagan classical tradition in which they had received their education, however much fire Christian polemicists, from Tertullian to Jerome, might choose to pour on it.

So too the culture, as well as the learning of pagan Rome, survived the change of faith made by the empire at the start of the fourth century. Thus the 'invisible world' that Mango describes the Byzantine Christian as inhabiting, turns out to be equally the property of pagan belief. In Peter Brown's memorable analogy, the world of demons was as real to the late Roman as that of bacterial microbes is to us – watch any advert for loo-cleaner if you are not sure!

When the early Church came along we see the failure – despite the proclamation of a unitary godhead – of the Christian attempt to abolish pluralist demonologies. Indeed an important Christian innovation – that of the saint – was explicitly considered to take his place alongside the forces of good against these. The custom of honouring the holy gives us a good illustration of how much the Church tried, and failed, to rein in such beliefs. Augustine's mother Monica was upbraided by St Ambrose (one saint by another!) for bringing offerings, in her provincial African way, to the shrine of a local Milanese saint.

At times it seemed as if a similar fate would befall the tradition of the *telonia* described, in varying degrees of academic curiosity and living fear, by Messrs Christos and Mango. Yet in spite of a deep suspicion on the part of Byzantine churchmen, it had survived. Furthermore, as I sat on the truckle-bed of my cell, distracted from time to time by the beauties of the coastline through my window, I remembered that the same men of simple faith had argued and prayed for its survival, for as long as there had been talk of *telonia* in the courtyards and on the balconies of the Holy Mountain.

*

After four days at the Lavra, Theoliptos summoned me to discuss my prospective tour of the peninsula. Accordingly, I spent the whole of Compline, and much of the social time afterwards, drawing up a detailed itinerary to set before my host when we met in the *archondariki*. I even appended a map. Theoliptos nodded encouragingly as I recited the name of each monastery where I intended to stay a night. Some of the distances were quite long, but revising the thing would be a difficult job.

When I completed the list, Theoliptos gave a sharp backward thrust of the head – that imperious Greek gesture of negation. He pushed the map away, and said, 'Matthaios, do not make plan!' At this moment he raised his right hand and looked up over his shoulder towards it. 'Go where . . . go where the Spirit tells you.' As he pronounced the word, he moved his hand suddenly skyward. 'If you like a place, stay there for a few days; if not go somewhere else. But listen to what the Spirit says inside your heart.'

I kept the map but buried it in a pile of books. It has given me a good laugh several times since.

CHAPTER 3

To Kavsokalivion

Why had I come to Athos? As I sat in my room, a keen breeze seeped through the casement window. I looked out towards the troubled sea. Often this stretch of the northern coast is too stormy to navigate, even in late summer, and the boat is unable to leave from Ierissos. But that, I remembered now, was the world beyond. Few miles but oceans of difference now separated us. Why was I stranded on the wrong side of this divide, the barrier between two worlds, a sea that had been sailed by but a handful since Byzantium? Why was I here, in this place so far from all the 'normality' for which, in a moment of sudden panic, I now longed?

I suppose I went to Athos out of curiosity. Since I am not Orthodox, the notion of going there on pilgrimage came to me slowly, in the wake of my first enthusiasm for what I hoped would be an exotic adventure. Yet the notion had taken shape, and so, by the end of my trip, I realized I was as much of a pilgrim as those whose religious credentials were more of a piece with the eastern faith of the Mountain. In one sense, as I was to discover, my own journey was in its own way quite possibly more of a pilgrimage than the trips made by some.

Such thoughts came later. In the first place, beyond the siren beckonings of foreign ways, I felt I could lay claim to 'a genuine interest in monasticism'. That had been Phillip Schofield's criterion when he placed his advertisement in *The Bridge* all those months before. I and one other had replied, and he had concluded I was the more worldly. An odd reason for choosing me perhaps, since that is rarely of much help when it comes to surviving on the Mountain.

What other reasons were there? I suppose my sense of history was awakened by the promise of strange scenes and vistas, not to mention the rituals and characters I knew I would find on Athos. All these I read about with growing excitement, and in some cases alarm, in the months leading up to my visit. All turned out to be based on an even stranger reality. The Mountain may be prosaic at times, but at others it is as wild and as mysterious as you could wish. As you walk through the silence of nature there, it can seem a peaceful place, yet somehow there is often a hint of danger. Where did this come from, I often wondered, as I made my way through undergrowth on a cliff-side path, or deeper into some forest.

The monks who have lived on Athos down the ages have tried, dedicatedly, to build a model of holiness out of their own thoughts, feelings and deeds – in other words, out of nothing more promising than the human will expressing itself through action, albeit channelled through the medium of prayer. In the midst of so many lives dedicated to God, how many remnants of other lives – lives left behind, or never lived – must have crowded the heads of Athos' monks down the centuries? Was it these longings, unprocessed, or broken on the altar of faith, that began to disturb me from the moment I ventured out into their territory alone?

These things are hard to understand; perhaps, they must remain opaque even through the whole of a monastic life.

Yet if we miss the tension, do we not also miss the very point of that life? I felt, while on Athos, that somehow I was in dialogue with many ways of thinking about the world, as if the representatives of many insights – no doubt some obsessions too – had found a way to voice their thoughts in my head from time to time. I found myself becoming peculiarly receptive to these thoughts, unafraid of what strange preoccupations the place was bringing out in me.

Was I, in a sense, simply losing it? My tour of the mountain on foot was now about to begin in a few hours. When on that tour I experienced these dialogues, this parade of thoughts – about home, about where I was going to work in inner-city Manchester, about my family and others close to me in my life – it was as if several hours' walking through the intense Greek noon-day heat had brought my mind closer to the essence of these things than I could ever imagine being in the midst of them. This, I suspect, is the paradox of asceticism which ends up being its whole point. By quitting the world, we come to understand it with a fresh set of senses, with a new heart even, as we could never understand if we were still immersed in it.

So it is, as Thomas Merton saw, that the actual practices of the ascetic life – the fasts and the renunciations – are far from being the object of that life. I am sure this has confused many who have embarked on the ascetic journey, those who have thought that an over-scrupulous anxiety will lead them to God. I would not be surprised either if many of these people, sadly, got almost nowhere towards the true goal of asceticism, even as they lived the outward form of monastic life. And yet paradoxically, the practices themselves remain important. When we abandon ourselves to new rhythms of eating and sleeping, as well as praying, we find many of the concerns we tend to think of as absolute necessities, the 'realities' of our world, just fall away. In the silence, we start to notice – perhaps it would be better to say remember – what is real.

It cannot be a coincidence that so many self-help books ask us to start by putting more space in our lives, to slow down, or to do normal things differently. When we make this effort – stopping to hold doors for people, not always trying to be the first in the queue – we are doing no more and no less than the self-same thing monks attempt: changing the basic practices of our lives. The ultimate goal may be to draw closer to God, but we get there by first exercising (as the Greek word *askesis* would have it) our humanity in a different way. When we make this start, we quickly find our inner perceptions change. No longer are the people around us merely obstacles in our way; rather, we come to see that by casting them in this light, they are forced to take on that role in our lives. Instead of fuming at their incursion into our territory, we step aside and let them go first – and so become part of the answer to their needs. What is more, in providing this for them, we provide it also for ourselves.

So much of this aspect of asceticism – what it has to offer to the world – has been forgotten in the torrent of criticisms which has deluged the ascetic life down the ages. These criticisms have concentrated on its mortifications and on the self-abandonment that is apparently, pointlessly, enjoined by that life. Yet the monk's positive connection with the world is ultimately as much a part of his devotion to God as any disavowal of himself. In a sense, the monk tries to achieve his own right relation to the world, in order finally to help that world in its own self-realization. This may involve setting an example for the charity that people in the world need to practise towards each other. Above all, the monk devotes himself to learning the ways of peace, so the same peace may spread out into the world from the monastery. How, though, is the monk to forge this right relation? How is he to connect the peace and charity which, ideally, is realized by his life in community, with the needs and experience of lives in the world beyond?

On one level, it has been thought that the monk need only pray for the peace of the world; on another that he needs to be engaged, actively and directly, with the problems faced within it. The problem, which goes back to all the monastic debates concerning action and contemplation, and further still to the interplay of these themes in Christian thought, will never go away. As soon as it does, something like the false isolation against which Thomas Merton warned will have crept into the heart of the monastic life.

Back in the fourth century, there sprang up a great interest in the holy life, as it was lived beyond the bounds of normal society. Pilgrims to Jerusalem would often make a detour, on their way home, to take in the centres of ascetic life which had sprung up throughout Egypt. There they would find a whole range of models of the ascetic life. As on Athos, lone anchorites struggled with inner temptations, in isolated cells scattered throughout the desert. At the same time, various types of community life had sprung up, from the large-scale monasteries founded by St Pachomius, to the smaller lavra-type communities directed by St Basil. What is important, concerning the connections between each of these models and the world at large, is that monastics everywhere, both male and female, continued to depend on that world. This remained true, however much they might seek to cultivate their own spiritual isolation.

A fertile interdependence, between world and cell, comes through strongly in the account of the lives of the first monks, provided by the ancient sources. Monks offered goods to the world: spiritual counsel in return for basic material sustenance. The materials might be food, or hemp for the manual work that was considered an essential part of their life. The two-way trade, in ideas and objects, is one of the great themes of the earliest monastic life, and so the desert cells were never without contact with the world, whether through the guests or the traders with whom they had constant dealings. As a result of this trade, the need came to decide two things: on the one hand, how far to allow the world into the desert; and, on the other, to what extent should monks go out from monastery or cell to help the world.

Pachomius found the second issue particularly difficult. Starting out as a soldier in the Roman army, the future saint had come into contact with a group of local Christians. Before long he had given up his military career, left his billet and begun caring for the sick of the town. It was at this point the call of the desert first reached into his life. Hearing of some Christians who had severed all links with society, he came to find even the charitable work he was doing a source of frustration. In one version of the life of the saint, he is heard raising his voice to heaven, asking to be rid of his burden and to have it fall on other shoulders. Eventually, Pachomius realized he had a choice to make, between direct acts of service, and the life of withdrawal in the desert. He chose the desert but the *Coptic Life* adds an interesting coda. Pachomius went on working with the poor for a further two years before leaving for the monastic life.

In that same *Life*, the founder of coenobitism was definite about the psychological and spiritual border that must run between his community and the world. As the head of a federation of monasteries, Pachomius went to great lengths to legislate on the required degrees of separation between the two. In general, monks were not to cross this border, even in order to help the world beyond. But such a separation has not seemed right to all monks at all times. As we have seen, traffic between monastery and world was a classic locus of early ascetic spirituality. In the sources, the Desert Fathers are seen, on occasions, upbraiding the traders with whom they came into contact, as well as fleeing and fighting animals – and drawing constructive lessons from the experience – not to mention disputing with bands of robbers. Yet after all this activity, there was the constant need to get back to the peace of solitude. 'Go sit in your cell,' said one monk, 'and your cell will teach you everything.'

Pachomius' contemporary, St Basil, could never quite believe this advice, and in this respect belongs to a different spiritual tradition. Before the time of the coenobium, the archetypal ascetic was a lone figure who championed the rights of the dispossessed and marginalized – righting wrongs, intervening with landowners, fighting corruption and its effects on the poor – just as modern ascetics may fight social exclusion in the inner city of today. Basil too became one of the great voices of the patristic period to speak out against such wrongs, and chose to develop his own network of monasteries dedicated to what in the Jewish tradition would be called *tikkun olam*, repairing the world. These communities – Basiliads as they became known – contained not only accommodation for the monks themselves, but also hospices, along the lines of a later medieval model: combined infirmaries and shelters for the homeless.

Basil believed passionately that the work of each hospice was not an adjunct to his monasteries, but a central part of them. The dual focus of these communities – action and contemplation – would become the foundation of Basil's later theology of the ascetic life. There, Basil argues that acts of service and prayer flow in and out of one another, via the heart of the contemplative who is at one with God. The principle for him was that as the monk ascended the ladder of contemplation, he should become ever more prepared to meet the needs of the world around. Even the two commandments identified by Jesus – to love God, and then one's neighbour as oneself – could obscure the interdependence between them. It was, for Basil, not a question of doing the first, and then the second. Instead, each made sense of the other.

When I went to Athos, I knew there had been a debate about such things within the ascetic life, as indeed within Christianity in general. But how far does the spiritual depend on the external, and how far do the two conflict? 'Faith without works is dead', wrote St James, while St Paul calls Christians to be 'in the world but not of it'. Is there a conflict here? Should Christians withdraw to bear witness to the second of these ideas, or does that risk prejudicing the first? One medieval abbot, Bernard Tolomei, kicked his entire group of monks out the front door of their Sienese monastery, to have them tend victims of the plague in the valley below. When I came to Athos, it was in part to learn how present-day monks might feel about possible conflicts between keeping their distance from and serving the world. Would Blessed Bernard's solution to the dilemma be their own?

*

The next morning Theoliptos banged on my door at about five o'clock. Did I want to make an early start before the sun became too hot? 'No thank you,' I called back as politely as possible in the circumstances.

Some minutes later, stirring awake, I remembered my host's piece of advice the previous evening: travel light, 'just a few clothes, nothing else'. Accordingly, I set about stuffing a good proportion of my wardrobe and a library of books into my deceptively capacious rucksack. I walked out the front gate of the Lavra with far too much on my back, but at least I was psychologically prepared for the ordeal which was to follow.

As soon as I gained the road leading through the Lavra's hinterland of ramshackle outbuildings with their workshops and animals, a pair of enormous gadflies locked onto my scent. Each hovering a continuously held distance of two feet from either ear, they sussurated with a happy, threatening hum. After some moments preparing their attack-plan, they peeled off one after the other to dive-bomb my cricket hat.

Gadflies are known for their tenacity once they have found something they want to sting. On my last visit to Greece, just before the Gulf War, my ferry was 'buzzed' in the middle of the Adriatic by a couple of Greek Air Force fighter-jets. Gadflies are far worse. My glasses still bore the marks of the last attack I had suffered at Priene in western Turkey. Since I was forced to jettison them onto the hard stone of the *bouleterion*, the ancient council-chamber, the two large craters in the lenses remained as warnings of what not to do when faced with these dastardly creatures.

Fortunately, as I have discovered on frequent trips to the Mediterranean, even gadflies have an Achilles heel. They respond to the flailings of any would-be victim, which is why when Hera had the hapless Io turned into a cow, her swishing tail was enough to get her pursued to the ends of the earth. One story is she leapt off a cliff in despair, and this is very easy to understand once you have been attacked. All these experiences are proof positive that you really do need to travel to classical lands in order to be a classicist.

On my outing to the skete of Prodromou, a couple of days before, I had perfected my resistance technique. It seems to be infallible and has served me well across many miles of walking in Greece. First you must maintain forward motion with a minimum of superfluous movement. Your assailant should then lose interest after about thirty seconds, although sometimes it takes about a minute, before making a timely end of its harassment. On occasions things take a little longer, but you must never, never struggle, since you won't escape, except by motorized transport, and possibly not even then. In fact I have seen these things fly alongside car windows at 20–30 mph. So true are these devils to their mythological paradigm, that any attempt to beat them away will only result in torments of a catastrophic order. After my friend and I were beset in Priene, it was the turn of our once-laughing fellow-tourists. Soon, I am sorry to say, they laughed no longer.

So, doused in insect-repellent and gliding as smoothly as possible along the dirt track, both arms motionless at my side, I headed south-west, bound once more for the skete of John the Baptist a couple of miles on from the Lavra. The saint's epithet, by which the community is known – Prodromou, meaning 'forerunner' – is such a marvellous one, focusing so precisely on John the Baptist's role in history. Prodromou was once one of the grander sketes, and a dependency of the Russian monastery, Ayiou Pateleimonos, which I was to visit later on. Now it is governed by the Lavra, in whose district it lies.

At Prodromou, a handful of monks live in what is but the shell of a once-thriving community. Perhaps things will change over the next few years, since for a while now, the number of postulants coming to Athos has been on the increase. Indeed, despite rumours, there were signs of more active habitation than at the Russian, and the guesthouse into which I glanced seemed impressively modern. A monk came up quickly to ask me what I needed.

*

At such moments – my engagement proper with monastic hospitality, and not the idealized hearsay of all I had read – I still did not exactly know what to expect. While at the Lavra I had felt, in a strange way, officially part of the community. I had been there already almost a week, and had found my feet in the monastic scheme of things. As well as my work with Christos and Theoliptos, who had taken me on a tour of some of the outhouses, I found myself with a couple of hours most afternoons to while away, pottering around my quarters in the *archondarikion*. I practically had my own suite, and was struggling not to grow complacent, sinking into a routine that sometimes seemed so easy I was beginning to wonder where the privations of solitude really began. I need not have worried since noon-day *accidie*, a combination of boredom and frustration, is well-documented by the first monastic writers. It would come to me, as to all, given time – perhaps my feelings now were only the beginning. For the time being, though, I was simply glad of my rest.

The monastic day intertwines periods of work and prayer, not to mention the meals that are so important. Soon

I had begun to find my own rhythm within this pattern. After lunch was over and my work with one of the others duly completed, I would retire to my cell to read and ponder. Did I pray as well? Less than I expected, perhaps, though probably more than I imagined at the time. Besides, much of the time on Athos seems to be its own sacred space anyway, either because formal prayer-times are so frequent, or because of a more profound numinousness pervading the Mountain. At the same time, part of this space came to life through the thoughts I had as I reflected on what I was experiencing, and as I linked what I had read and studied to these.

Another thing that helped me to feel at home, as well as part of the structure, was my own role in providing hospitality. Whenever new guests came to the guesthouse, they would need to be shown the ropes. It was not really high season yet, since it was only later in the month that several hundred pilgrims would pass through the Lavra in the course of a week. Yet those that did come needed to be shown how to make their coffee, and at this I became quite adept.

In the *archondarikion* there was a tiny stove, and on this you placed a hand-held pot with exactly the right proportions of water and coffee, all of it very well sugared. Waiting till the whole thing boils over, and then catching the overflow is an art and it is this that becomes your cup of coffee. No French person would ever boil their coffee, but on Athos this, it seems, is *de rigueur*. Once the coffee was made, some of the most peaceful moments of the day would ensue, as you took your cup and sat with it in silence. It was a silence that might be punctuated by a casual comment, though it never quite seemed to be broken. Such is the way of things in monasteries.

*

Now as I went up to the monk at Prodromou, I was conscious of being on the other side of the fence. Here it was I who was going to be welcomed. No longer in my element at the Lavra, I tried to stay calm and remember the appropriate bits of Greek. On Athos, such exchanges are never hurried, although they may be both discomfitingly and refreshingly direct. The odd prevarications of social speech really are a world away here.

'Greetings, Father.'
'Greetings to you. What is it you need? Perhaps some water?'
'Well, yes.'
'It's just here. Help yourself.'

And soon I was on my way.

*

From Prodromou, the path really becomes exciting. After a steep climb up through the wood above, I emerged onto a great seaward slope. Trees cascaded down to the rocky shoreline a hundred feet below, while a continuous serenade of nesting birds and cicadas accompanied this vision of age-less tranquillity. I halted to rest my feet and eyes. Shortly afterwards, the path which threaded its way across this incline suddenly divided. The lower was signed for the skete of Kavsokalivion, the upper to that of Ayias Annas, other-wise known as St Anne's. It was decision time.

On the way from Prodromou I had passed a pair of pil-grims. They were father and son – a frequent combination on the Mountain. The son could not have been more than eleven or twelve, and was certainly a bare-faced youth. Such pilgrimages are presumably something of a rite of passage in

Orthodox Greece. How far had they come to make theirs, I wondered – from Athens? From the Peloponnese? I had not stopped to disturb them, but now that I was landed with a choice, I considered waiting for them to catch up – just on the off-chance that their map might be better than mine. I knew, from a previous conversation, they were headed for Ayias Annas, which lies a couple of miles inland. According to my own poor pilgrim guide, the path should cut away roundabout here, to leave the coast and its spectacular views. Not really sure of the Spirit, I decided to follow the inland fork. In the end it did not matter – with typical Athonite quirkiness, the paths rejoined a couple of hundred yards later.

What I needed most of all – much more than the compass I had brought with me – was the Austrian contour-map, the Zwerger. I ought to have picked one up at Ouranopoli, since they do not actually sell them on the Mountain. But was this the Spirit after all? With a Zwerger in my pocket, I would never have made the fortunate mistake I now in fact made.

Abandoning my fellow pilgrims to their inland track I continued along the coast. The view was still spectacular, when I glimpsed it from frequent breaks in the dense wood which here, as almost everywhere on the peninsula, virtually covers the slope. Finally I emerged to find the path taking a nose-dive down towards the shore. For at least a mile it snaked back and forth across what was, when I checked a friend's Zwerger map later, a preposterous gradient for a path.

Stupidly, there were other omissions in my kit. For an obscure reason, which I can only relate to the self-abandonment that is a vital part of the pilgrim experience, I

53

had omitted to bring my walking-boots. By the end of the path I was turning my ankles at every step. To make things worse, the rocks on either side threw the glare and heat straight back at me, and so, after an hour's struggle, I reached a shady plateau only a paltry distance beneath where I had started. I sank down on my pack completely exhausted. Relief, though, was in sight. Below, the roofs of a hamlet peeped out between the trees and shrubs at the foot of the slope. This must, finally, be Kavsokalivion!

Dropping down the rest of the path, I found the central building of the skete. A two-storey affair, the lower floor housed a stable and tool shed, into which I peeped, hoping to stumble across the monks. Next door, the beds in the single storey guesthouse could just be made out through windows that were very grimy – an odd detail, since most guestquarters are kept spectacularly clean. Then I found the sign – *Hora Hesuchias* (hour of rest) 12 to 3 – and realized it was going to be a long wait before my would-be hosts reappeared.

Retiring to the shade of a tree, in the kitchen-garden below the buildings, I unshouldered my pack and sat down to read. At 3 o'clock prompt, a long white beard poked itself over the balcony of the house. Was this Kavsokalivion?, I enquired. Again, the long slow drawing back of the head announced my mistake. No, this was Ayiou Dimitriou, Kavsokalivion being a good half-hour further on, round the next headland. But I ought to make it there, if not as far as Ayias Annas. Reluctantly I bid the beard *kalli mera* and set off once more.

*

Leaving Kavsokalivion two days later I knew I had uncovered the wisdom of Theoliptos' advice. Could the Spirit have led me to a better place? Here, surely, was the heart of Athos. I came in along the side of the valley to catch my first glimpse of this amazing settlement, where it falls away from its main church – the *kiriakon* – at the very top. From here down to the sea, tier on tier of tiny dwellings spread down the precipitous slope. It would be a long way up to that *kiriakon* on Sundays.

That is when the community would meet for worship, since Kavsokalivion – which I had reached in just over an hour – is an idiorrythmic community of painters and artisans. In this picturesque hamlet lay-workers, as at the Lavra, outnumber the monks in their usual black habits and monastic caps. If anything though, dress is much less formal here. When you see photographs of Athos monks in faded garb – roughened by long toil down the years – the chances are they will be hermits or else, as here, members of a semi-eremitic community.

Arriving at the topmost level of the village, I made my way straight over to the church. I had read that in idiorrhythmic communities, you will find a guesthouse adjoining the *kiriakon* itself. Sure enough, in the courtyard I stumbled into the corpulent monk of a certain age who was to look after me for the next couple of days. Friar Tuck, as he was soon known to my diary, was a kind and hospitable man with whom I soon became friends.

Friar Tuck's own story was intriguing. He had been a monk in several of the major monasteries, and it seems that moving from one to another, in search of one's spiritual home, is a common experience. Having lived at Kavsokalivion for the past five years, he knows that now he is where he is supposed to be. All day he works around the house, preparing supper in the kitchen, which doubles as guesthouse refectory, for his partner and whosoever may happen to turn up. It struck me as a peaceful thought that for all the time since I first went to college in 1988, he had swept this same floor that I was sweeping now. How many meals must he have cooked with visitors like me?

Soon I was on culinary detail. And it was not just for me and the monks that I waded through the vegetables. In the two days I spent there, we were joined at the *archondariki* table first by a pair of elderly, faintly grumpy, pilgrims as well as by a young Albanian teenager, who had come to be baptized. The others tested him diligently on his creed as I chopped my way through a bowl of onions.

Although it was tiny, the *archondariki* had the customary library-table littered with a jumble of books on Orthodox spirituality and history. That night, I picked one that looked promising and was so impressed that I made a note, determining to write to Bishop Kallistos about it. The book was Alexander Schmemann's *For the Life of the World: Sacraments and Orthodoxy* – written for American youths, but a rich exposition in anyone's language.

*

Athonite spirituality itself is strongly in the mystical tradition. Early on, the Holy Mountain became the cradle of a movement called hesychasm. The Neo-Platonic writers who supported this movement developed a so-called 'apophatic' or 'negative' theology in the light of which they tried to approach God by stripping away all extraneous layers of conscious experience – language, sense impressions, mundane thoughts, and so on. To this end, they developed rigorous and complex breathing techniques, some of which I was to have demonstrated to me by an eager Italian tourist later on.

The problem came, however, with the endpoint. The hesychasts claimed to be able to see a vision of God at the summit of their mystical experience. This claim sparked a furious controversy in the eastern Church, every bit as internecine as that between iconoclasm and the iconodules. In the end, after much wrangling, it took some nice distinctions by the brilliant theologian St Gregory Palamas to quell the storm. Writing in the fourteenth century, Palamas explained that what the hesychasts saw could be considered the uncreated light of God, rather than his actual substance. Everyone, almost, was happy.

There are some serious issues here. In a sense the spiritual ascent of hesychasm is dangerously close to dualism, locating as it does, in very Platonic terms, the authentic experience of the pilgrim in the world as something that is fundamentally disconnected from that world. Such a notion should not, strictly speaking, form any part of orthodox Christian thought, since in the Gospel we come to know God precisely through our service to others, through the Jewish ideal of loving our neighbour.

The problem is that without an enlightened structure like the Basiliad, it does not seem possible to do both, to be active in charity as well as engaged in the mystical ascent of contemplative prayer. This problem has run through many a debate within Christianity about the proper role of Christians in this world, whether it is the first arguments about the authority of the Roman empire, or those over liberation theology.

On the mystical side, the pilgrim ascends through a series of peaks in contemplative experience to arrive at the knowledge of God, the vision, for example, of the hesychasts. The process is essentially about forgetting one's feet of clay – to move beyond the stage where one is still grounded emotionally, as well as physically, in the world of the temporal. This project informs the *raison d'être* of Athos as a place where the world can be forgotten, even to the point of replacing the reality of physical generation.

Recently, I was not surprised to find an echo of this spirituality in Bishop Kallistos' account of his experience when, as the seventeen-year-old Timothy Ware, he stumbled into an Orthodox church.

It was a hot summer's afternoon and I was wandering aimlessly through the streets of London when I saw a church I had never been inside before. My first impression was that the building was completely empty. As my eyes became accustomed to the gloom I noticed there were a few people standing near icons with burning lamps in front of them. Somewhere out of sight a choir was singing. After a little while, the deacon emerged from the sanctuary to sing one of the litanies. My first impression of emptiness was now succeeded by a quite different impression: I felt that the church was packed with worshippers I couldn't see but who were playing an immediate and dynamic part in our prayer. I had a feeling that this quite simple service was in fact heaven on earth. A good deal later when I'd read more about Orthodoxy, I realized that this idea of heaven on earth is fundamental to the whole approach of the Orthodox Church towards worship. And I can remember that when I emerged from the church and suddenly came out into the sun and light and heard again the sound of the traffic, it was as if I had been on another level of reality, and I had no idea how long I'd been in there, whether it was five minutes or two hours.

Interview with Bishop Kallistos in *The Door*, September 1993

Yet Kallistos is alive to the tensions here, and tries convincingly to explain how the mystical tradition of prayer can operate practically in one's life – not just as an arcane diversion from it.

> I think of a phrase of the great Romanian Orthodox priest Father Dumitru Staniloae. He says there are as many different ways of loving God as there are different persons. The Holy Spirit speaks to each one of us in our uniqueness, in our distinctive particularity. I see both marriage and monasticism as sacraments of love. In both cases we are expressing our love for God. No one should ever become a monk or nun unless they also have a real sense of the value of marriage as a source of grace and sanctification. And married people also need to have a sense of the value of dedicated celibacy.

The same issues come up again and again in the history of monasticism. How can one really be there for the world, for one's neighbour, if one is secluded in one's convent? How can marriage be valued by priests and religious when it is the very thing they renounce?

It was in the fourth century that battle really commenced, on the second of these issues, although tensions had been bubbling from the time of St Paul onwards. An urbane young monk called Jovinian decided, after considerable ascetic experience, that the rigours of his personal regime were in fact an irrelevance when it came to his relationship with God. (This is certainly a familiar argument.) In order to correct what he saw as the imbalance in his former views, he decided to abandon most of his ascetic practices, and took to living what his supporters considered to be a harmoniously integrated life in the midst of the city. Among other things, he went to the baths again, and fraternized with a range of people, even women.

The ascetic Church, which was very sizeable by now, was horrified. Some friends of Jerome got together to collect evidence about Jovinian's new lifestyle and nefarious views, and dispatched their reports to the great scholar. Jerome went through the roof. In a fulminating attack, he excoriated the ex-monk – who nevertheless appears, in fact, to have stuck to his chaste lifestyle – for bringing a holy institution into disrepute. Attacking Jovinian on every conceivable score (most widely exaggerated, as scholars now believe) Jerome ended his tirade with an attack on marriage itself. In a memorable slur, he even went as far as to suggest that for the married martyr, the blood of their martyrdom was not enough to wash away the stain of the marriage bed. Now it was Jerome's friends' turn to be horrified. An attempt was made to gather in all the saint's pamphlets, and copies were sent to Augustine in his north African diocese of Hippo.

Augustine straightaway had a problem. He did not want to offend or discourage those who had taken his own advice and followed the evangelical 'counsels of perfection'. Yet neither could he sit by while another Christian institution was disparaged. The invective had got out of hand, and Jerome, ever the extremist, needed to be brought back into line.

Augustine's response became a classic. At the same time as he lauded the ascetic choice to the stars, he established marriage itself as a substantive good of human, and in particular Christian, life. Strongly attacking its detractors – with some significant nods in the direction of St Jerome – he also harangued those who found fault with consecrated virginity. At the same time Augustine's tract, *On the Good of Marriage*, set up the threefold account of its virtues that was to be transmitted down centuries of Christian tradition. Aquinas himself followed it, and it survives to this day as a basic model of reference for Christian thinking on the subject.

What even Augustine – a friend of marriage, despite his own tumultuous experiences – would not accept, however, was the equality of this state with that of consecrated virginity. If both were goods, there was still a hierarchy of perfection, with the prize belonging to the virgin. In fact the notion of the superiority of virginity – understood, technically, not as physical virginity, but as consecrated dedication to celibacy – survives to this day in the catechism of the Catholic Church. There consecrated virginity is described as 'the unfolding of baptismal grace' and given an explicitly higher status than marriage.

Many Christians I know – including several who believe there is a point to the ascetic project, some being celibates themselves – disagree strongly with this teaching. Both marriage and virginity are for them simply two separate ways to God, each with its own set of charisms.

Neither of these, it is true, should be undervalued. For me, one of the key charisms of the consecrated life is that of availability towards others – especially to the poor and marginalized. In her book, *Dead Man Walking*, the American nun Helen Préjean discusses this theme with an inmate of Death Row, whom she has been comforting through his ordeal, even as she fights against the injustices of the system. Yet when it gets round to a conversation about her personal life, she is challenged by his suspicion of her celibacy. In response to his honest questions, Préjean observes that if she had a husband and family, she would probably be back home with them now – round the barbecue on a sunny Sunday afternoon – and not sitting next to him inside a prison.

*

As I sat of an evening on the *archondarikion* balcony at Kavsokalivion, watching the beauty of an Aegean coastline at dusk, the simple dwellings of the hamlet at peace on the slope beneath me, all such tensions within religious life were far from my mind. Rather that day, the words that I read seemed, as they always did on Athos, to flow in and out of my conversations with those around.

I had been sitting earlier on my bed when Friar Tuck cracked open the door and, for a reason beyond my ken, launched into a description of the Jesus prayer. It was about this prayer, and its mantra – 'Lord Jesus, Son of the Living God, have mercy on me' – that I had been reading moments before.

Serendipity continued to merge with the peace of this place all through my stay at Kavsokalivion, definitely the home of the Spirit. As I lay on my truckle-bed in Friar Tuck's *archondarikion*, I cast my mind forward to the next morning. Then the entire inhabitants of this skete would wend their way up to the *kiriakon* beside us here at the top of the hill, to gather for their Sunday worship. With this holy thought, I promptly fell asleep on my copy of Alexander Schmemann.

*

The next morning I joined the community of Kavsokalivion in church. Back at the Lavra I had spent several hours watching and listening to the liturgy from my misericord in the rear wall of the narthex, where I had begun to pick up a little of the ritual – bowing to the censer as he glides past your stall, standing and sitting at the appropriate times. Not comprehending the words, I made my own private prayer, and allowed the tranquil ceaseless chanting to flow into my mind. I had made a habit of settling into the same seat – one nearest the aisle, from which I could get the best view through to the nave and the sanctuary beyond. I had begun, too, to feel like one of the community as I gazed round at the newly arrived pilgrims stifling their 5 am yawns. Now finally in Kavsokalivion, I was a pilgrim proper myself.

CHAPTER 4

The Hanging Convents

Moving on from Kavsokalivion was difficult. The last morning, it was with some sadness that I stood in the kitchen cum guesthouse, to have my photo taken alongside the young Albanian and Friar Tuck. One of the elderly pilgrims stepped in to do the honours. Minutes later I would begin my descent, in company with the same Greek gentleman and his friends, down to the village *arsanas*. I resolved then, if I ever came back to Athos, to return here to Kavsokalivion.

My final day in the skete had been a generally lazy one. I had walked down the hill through the jumble of monastic dwellings in search of an illicit swim. Unfortunately, the only beach I might have used was inaccessible without a spot of rock-climbing. Considering and even half-heartedly attempting this option, I quickly gave up for safety's sake, and decided instead to climb the gorge above the skete.

I wanted to see if I could make it to Kerasia, the skete that lies halfway between Kavsokalivion and Ayias Annas. By the time I was half an hour out, the mid-morning heat had defeated me. This heat is hardly the worst of the day on Athos, which tends to come after lunchtime. But it got the better of me entirely and so I sat down on a rock to read for an hour or so, before returning the way I had come. In case I was becoming endangered by a surfeit of spirituality, I had packed the right remedy – there is nothing quite like George Eliot for dissipating the atmosphere of the Holy Mountain. And so I returned to the world of Casaubon, and wondered about the *Key to All Mythologies*. On my way down, I was overtaken by a mule and its driver, the Athonite equivalent of a Porsche. Seeing is certainly believing when it comes to the speed of these things.

I felt no remorse about my upcoming boat trip away from Kavsokalivion. There were enough exertions to come. I planned later on to walk the strip of convents that leap out from the cliffs along the south coast of Mount Athos. These 'hanging monasteries' include the famous Ayiou Simonos Petras, familiarly abbreviated to Simonopetra. I realized I had made the right choice now to take the *kaiki*, as soon as the boat pulled away from the headland. Once out on the water, the view of Kavsokalivion was amazing – tier on tier of *kalyvai*, the whole village teetering at what seemed a stupendous angle down the cliff-face. The whole coastline indeed is dramatic. Along the stretch of headlands between here and Ayiou Pavlou it takes in many twists and turns of wooded gulleys. These would have made, as I knew now from my most recent outing on foot, for treacherously difficult progress. We made our way on past sketes and hermitages – a series of views as rewarding as that of Kavsokalivion, to arrive at our destination of Ayiou Pavlou, the convent of St Paul's, and the first monastery proper since I had left the Lavra to round the headland of Mount Athos itself.

At about nine in the morning we edged into the *arsanas*. Straightaway a lorry, like some infernal rollercoaster, shot us hair-raisingly up the mountainside. Drifting through the portals of Ayiou Pavlou, we were welcomed into the meal that was already in progress. Moments after we found our places, the reader's monotone halted abruptly, signalling the end of the meal. But now came the surprise. A monk brought a delicious cake of raisins and meal round to each table, depositing a spoonful into the outstretched napkin of every monk and pilgrim. Today was a feast and so the usual Monday fast was broken by a full-scale lunch with wine and the additional treat of this dessert.

There was a joyful atmosphere, hard to pin down – was it simply a matter of the feast? My late-arriving friends and I were disgorged into the courtyard, together with the rest of the community who promptly vanished. We hung around, waiting for the appearance of some guestmaster or other. We waited in vain. Perhaps, without our knowing it, some long and complex feastday rituals were coming protractedly to a close in some far off corner of the convent. Yet there were no other pilgrims to be seen either, no one who had arrived the day before.

I looked about. The place was forbiddingly cloistered, a tower of stone staring down at the sea and at the world beyond. Inside there was a friendlier, but still determinedly distant feel. Still there was no welcome in the offing, nor did the warren of corridors, even the one marked with an arrow to the *archondarikion*, seem anything but politely uninviting. I decided to press on.

Attacking the short but strenuous walk to the next monastery, I made my way up over the headland beyond Pavlou with some vigour. Certain once more I was not where I was supposed to be, I even steamed past a train of Italian yuppies, looking somewhat the worse for wear between their designer bandannas and hiking boots. Was I spurred on by envy of the latter? By the time they arrived at Ayiou

Dionisiou, I was halfway through the book I had picked up in the guesthouse there.

Sitting on a divan in the *archondarikion*, to which I had been shown by the kindly guestmaster, I set aside my book to take in the glad sight of the *loukoumi* and *ouzo*, the universal welcome on the Holy Mountain. It is amazing how oriental in their luxury seem the guesthouses of Athos, after the sparseness of everything else there. A few soft cushions and books, and all is right with the weary traveller – this one anyway. Strange, too, to be met at the heart of Athos by a monk fluent in English and to be shown straightaway more wisdom from Bishop Kallistos, a man I might have quizzed about the Orthodox holy life back in his Oxford study. Now at least I could read with some understanding of the life lived in this most withdrawn of holy sites.

Ayiou Dionisiou was the first and perhaps the best of my stops on this tour, after Kavsokalivion. The next morning I stood on the *archondariki* roof, beside the domes of the *katholikon*, looking up at the peak of Mount Athos itself whose ruddy penumbra announced the dawn. There were other delights here, from the beautiful frescoes in the church and refectory to the gentle welcome of the guestmaster and the immaculate dormitories of his *archondarikion*. There was to be finer, more impressive architecture in other places on my tour, yet how often this would be marred by the human dimension of a place.

As my tour continued, I came to be annoyed – perhaps mutually – over what seemed to me, a lack of concern for the non-Orthodox. By the end I found myself progressively less tolerant of those convents where we were left out of both meals and services. On the other side, it is precisely because I had felt the warmth of an open welcome at enough establishments, that I failed to see how making allowances with strangers – for lacking the true faith, for being foreign – need compromise the piety of a place. Perhaps some convents have had bad experiences, but there is surely some virtue in offering visitors an opportunity to prove themselves.

At Dionisiou, Orthodox pilgrims sit at a different table from the community while their non-Orthodox associates occupy a third. Elsewhere I was to have the full range of experiences from full integration at one end, to being let into a cold and empty refectory, after the egress of everyone else, to find my food cooling on the table. It had been left there since, I presumed, the very beginning of the meal. Monks cleared around me as I made my lonely repast. Who was the more Christlike then, I wondered dourly. That experience, together with another during a service, must rank as the most dismaying occurrence on the Holy Mountain, as much at the level of ecumenism as simple hospitality. There was no such problem at Dionisiou, a holy place and friendly, where I slept very well that night.

The next morning saw my worst loss of temper on the Holy Mountain. No one suffered for it, much as I wished they had. Since the walk beyond Dionisiou threatened to be as arduous as the path above Pavlou the previous day, I decided when I left the convent gates next morning, to go down and wait for the boat. A monk in the guesthouse informed me it would arrive at ten. After this time had come and gone, I asked the two young Greek guys waiting with me where they were heading. The answer was the opposite direction. Even so, I reckoned the best plan would be to check which way the *kaiki* was going, when it arrived.

In the end this did not seem necessary. Moments before the boat drew alongside the *arsanas*, a reliable-looking whitebeard came pacing down the road. When I asked him where the boat was headed, he explained that the others were right, it would be going back to Pavlou. Therefore there was nothing else to do but face the onward walk in the gathering mid-morning heat. I turned away from the quay as undejectedly as possible, resigned to making the best of it. The old monk duly met his friend and waved goodbye to me.

Then the unimaginable happened. Casting a glance back to the departing *kaiki*, it became all too clear which way the boat was going – straight back along the coast to Dafni via that day's goal, Osiou Grigoriou! The old monk shrugged apologetically. When I continued to look at him for an explanation, my eyebrows arching involuntarily, he muttered something that did not seem overly anxious. Such things really are not important on Athos. I would learn humility, even if it took the vagaries of Athonite transport to teach it to me.

Unfortunately I had not quite reached the required level of wisdom, and so I stomped on angrily through the undergrowth. The path turned out to be the most difficult I had encountered. Climbing and climbing, it snaked its way up at an incline that was by now a familiar, if far from well-loved, challenge. My mind too began to take fanciful turns. Since both wolves and other wildcats cling on in the most mountainous stretches of Greece, I did not need to wait to be told to worry about their continued existence on Athos. On Athos such creatures, if they truly exist beyond the imaginings of travellers and monks, will still have to compete with the gun-toting national police. These it would seem like nothing better than to while away their time on Mount Athos, hunting the biggest quarry they are able to find. Since a tour of duty here is surely akin to Siberia, it is hard to blame them.

Nevertheless, it seemed wise to be prepared for anything. The stories of the Desert Fathers themselves are full of incidents with lions and jackals. How many monks today, as they make their way up to lonely woodland hermitages or to cliff-top eyries, must give just a little more than a passing thought to the perils that lurk in the undergrowth and behind the trees of modern Athos? Was I now to be prey to just such an untimely horror? The predatory intentions of any remaining jackals were dismissed by my guidebook, but somehow its air of dry inconsequence seemed too reminiscent of the traveller returned to be of much comfort at the moment. The undergrowth continued to bristle sinisterly on either side.

Amazingly, I reached Osiou Grigoriou within an hour albeit in a state of near exhaustion. Trying not to think too much about what had happened was difficult. My monkly adviser's lackadaisical concern for the details of the situation would prove typical of arrangements throughout my journey round Athos. The Spirit might lead me to the convent of Koutloumoussiou but would the gatekeeper know what that Spirit had in mind? That, however, is another story.

At Grigoriou – my third stop since the Lavra – I would surely be presented with the time-honoured welcome, already familiar enough for me to expect it enthusiastically. I could do, especially, with that thimbleful of *metaxa*. But it was not to be. With no guestmaster in sight I ended up being shown to a bed by a sympathetic fellow pilgrim of dubious authority in the matter. When I later reached Xenofontos and, recalling this fiasco, found my own way to my bed, I was sternly reproved by a group of Greek lads. It disconcerted me considerably till I realized they knew about as little as I did about the protocol. I at least had been on Athos a week!

My evening at Grigoriou was one of the most interesting, if not perhaps the most peaceful, I would spend on the Mountain. I have already mentioned how Athos is, for many, a way of coming home to Greek culture. This was undoubtedly true of the British Cypriot with whom I talked at length at this monastery. Yet his decision to settle on Athos was more than that. As the sun came down and the bats began to flit, this *dochimos* talked of the cynical attitude to sex that he had been drawn into in the secular society of London. My questions were twofold. Did he, Dimitrios, have to come here to renounce such an attitude? Furthermore, was sexuality really the most significant battle to be faced by the Christian soul? I wanted to know if he had found the peace for which he was looking. Where would that peace now be if he, or Christos for that matter, had stayed in their old jobs in the world that lay beyond Athos, and to where, I now remembered, I would soon myself be returning?

*

Renunciation of sex has always been far less central to eastern Christian asceticism than either its critics or some of its supporters have liked to pretend. St Antony the Great, a fourth-century Egyptian, is often heralded as the founder of Christian monasticism – even though it is clear from the *Life* of the saint that he was certainly not the first desert monk. When he first set out into the desert, it was not so much what he was leaving as what he was trying to discover that was on his mind. The path of ascetic wisdom is fundamentally about positives, about the new kind of person you can become, not what you choose to go without.

'Some men', writes Thomas Merton, 'have perhaps become hermits with the thought that sanctity could only be attained by escape from other men.' But escape, or rather escapism, can never be the way to Christian life.

If you go into the desert merely to get away from people you dislike, you will find neither peace nor solitude, you will only isolate yourself with a tribe of devils. True solitude is the home of the person, false solitude the refuge of the individualist.

For Merton, ascetic life is a matter of connecting, not separating: 'The only justification for a life of deliberate solitude is the conviction that it will help you to love not only God but also other men.' Other people are important, and so too are our own characters. If we go into the desert to flee from selfishness or anger, we will probably find that they are there in the desert already awaiting our arrival. It is there that the struggle actually begins.

*

My stay at Grigoriou was, as it happened, the occasion of my only deliberate infringement of law or custom on the Holy Mountain. I went for a swim! The one consolation of my hike from Dionisiou after the disaster at the *arsanas*, was that I had seen a perfectly hidden cove, as I made my way up onto the steep path bound for Grigoriou. If you must swim, warned my subversive guidebook, don't do it where anyone can see you (and never naked, it added cautiously). The next day I retraced my steps from Grigoriou to find myself standing, in a matter of minutes, on the tiny stretch of beach that was now all my heart's desire, preparing to take the plunge into the waters of recalcitrance. I swam briefly for fear that one of the vessels which plied the coast continuously might turn out to be a police launch. In fact I must have been far less conspicuous while swimming than when later I sat at the water's edge, in my bright yellow trunks, to read Baynes' *Byzantine Empire.* In the event the most common boats were tourist cruisers, loud hailing their way around the coast. There be women, I mused.

Exploring the edge of the cove, I stumbled across the mouth of a cave. But not only that. Here an old blanket seemed to have been lain out to dry. Even more intriguingly, a pile of household batteries were warming in the sun. What Walkman-wearing Philoctetes slept within? Had I stumbled on an out-of-the-way cell, in which some holy elder, a wizened *gerondas,* now sat watching me a few feet away within the darkness? I did not stay long to disturb his peace.

And so from asceticism, through frolics tinged with fear, to a story of some sadness. Grigoriou was proving to be a strange mixture. As I waited at the *arsanas* the last morning there, after my swim, I was joined by two young lads. One of them, the younger, seemed despondent. An Albanian Greek, he had come south to work for the summer. Having been promised pay he had so far received none and would have to stay a few more weeks to get it even as he desperately wanted to go home. His friend, a twenty-year-old student, seemed more hopeful. Nevertheless I was reminded that life on the borders of asceticism can be far from easy when you do not have the choice of living by its code, nor of renouncing luxury. The three of us talked for an hour or so while the *kaiki* made up its mind which way it was going.

In the end, to general disgruntlement, the boat headed back again to the north to pick up some of the passengers it had left behind, and so I took the opportunity to show my new friends some pictures of my girlfriend, and later to exchange addresses. Not for the last time I took a welcome dose of inter-rail culture, by way of antidote to the frequent intensity of the mountain, for as long as it was on offer.

Soon the boat returned to take us on to Dafni. I had circumnavigated Athos.

CHAPTER 5

North of Dafni

In recent years, the Russian Church has reversed its unilateral decision to admit Roman Catholics to communion. The measure never gained wide acceptance, nor had it been accepted by any of the other Orthodox churches. Everywhere I went during my stay on Athos, people expected I would be Catholic. When I arrived at the monastery of Xeropotamou, high in the hills above Dafni, I looked forward to discussing the reason for this as well as East–West church relations in general with one Brother Benedict. He was an English monk whom I knew from frequent reports to be resident there. Little did I know that neither today nor the next day would there be much to say.

Things started off well enough. Arriving at Dafni, the band of neophyte pilgrims, with me in their midst, stumbled ashore. While everyone else got their bearings, I repaired to the sole taverna for a quick cup of coffee, and to plan my next move. According to the sketchy map I possessed, the walk up to Xeropotamou was moderately challenging – a couple of miles, albeit in the noon-day heat along a steep enough climb. Setting off, I got into my stride fairly quickly, and was almost annoyed when a monk at the wheel of a large lorry screeched to a halt in a cloud of dust a few yards ahead of me. Flinging open the door, he beckoned to me to jump in, and in no time at all we pulled up at the gates of the monastery.

Arriving at Xeropotamou, I was received into the beautifully kept *archondariki* and given my refreshments by the guestmaster. Brother Benedict, clearly on call for such occurrences, had just finished talking to the other two British arrivals, and duly came over to me. He promised to see me for a few minutes the next morning to discuss Orthodoxy and the specific questions I had, and left me and my new companions to look around.

Xeropotamou is not a beautiful monastery, but it is striking. A huge unkempt courtyard surrounds the *katholikon*. Through the cracked pavement a myriad of weeds had sprung up. The buildings that stood on the four sides of the square seemed like large impersonal barracks, and a couple of them had been gutted by fire. The convent would have needed a couple of hundred monks to populate its wide unused spaces. Yet the frescoes in the refectory were attractive and interesting enough. Despite the general military feel, there was also a lovely pagoda, complete with benches from which I admired the view down the valley in the company of my two new British friends, Ian and David.

The hospitality, after that first hour, was disappointing. When my companions and I arrived at the church for the last portion of the pre-supper service, we were simply forbidden to enter. At other places, the church at these moments is open to all pilgrims whether Orthodox or not. Neither were we permitted to dine with the community, or even the other pilgrims, but instead had to wait till they had finished before being shown to our table. Indeed the next morning I was left feeling I had made a huge error, and had given Brother Benedict an embarrassing duty to perform.

Rising early, I crossed to the *katholikon*, and entered to an unfamiliar sight. The celebrating priests stood not in the sanctuary, but instead in the main body of the church, their vestments scintillating in the midst of a full congregation. Censers swung at their side, enveloping them in clouds as they intoned the morning hymns. After a few moments I caught the English monk's eye. He walked briskly over and led me from the building. Could I not sit at the back of the church? 'No,' he said, 'not now.'

In the Early Church, at moments of high solemnity – during the eucharist, for example – a curtain would be drawn to separate the baptized from the uninitiated, who could proceed no further than the narthex. Remaining at one remove from the congregation, they were separated from proceedings by a screen. Clearly I had stumbled in at just such a moment in the liturgy, and indeed I was never to see priests out of the sanctuary again. Yet being a visitor serious enough to want to attend the worship in the church did not seem to be any kind of qualification. Nor did I ever get to have my conversation with Brother Benedict after that.

When I met my fellow Brits again, two days later in Karies, they seemed to have performed even more dismally, in the offence stakes, than I had. Like me, they were left not quite knowing why. They were dismayed to learn the Lavra was my own base, for there they claimed to have been treated with great suspicion, and upbraided for, among other things, their clothing. I made some proprietorial apologies – surely it could not have been Theoliptos who was rude to them?

Nevertheless, in their muddling way, Ian and David perhaps got closer than I ever did to the heart of Athonite asceticism. Since they were dying for a swim, at

Xeropotamou I recounted my escapade on the shore between Dionisiou and Grigoriou, and directed them to the cove which had been the scene of my miscreancy. Beware the hermit, I warned. When I met up with the pair again, it seemed the joke was on me – there was a hermit living in the vicinity! In a decaying medieval tower, about a hundred yards away from the path, our intrepid tracksuit-wearing pilgrims had been plied with *ouzo* and *loukoumi*, of which, it would seem, hermits also keep a store.

The interconnections, between Ian's and David's tour of the Mountain and my own, did not stop there. Indeed it is one of the joys – and sometimes almost a mystery – that walking anywhere for great periods of time, fate seems to take you to places you would never have reached if you had stuck resolutely every moment to your original set of destinations. If this is true elsewhere, it is certainly true on Athos. Perhaps the feeling I had, that there it was even more the case, is due to the sharpened senses I started to develop in even a few days. Theoliptos would call it the Spirit, and I have known it in many of the regions, in Greece and other places where I have walked long distances. It relies wholly on an openness to the way you must take each day, and to the micro-deviations from the way which suggest themselves by frequent turns. This openness would mostly be ruined by having a car – as if on Athos that were even much of a practical advantage. Now as the paths of the three of us crisscrossed on the Mountain, it was happening again.

Ian's and David's lone monk was, originally, American. A day later I would run into him myself, even as I made the choice between two routes. As I stepped onto a boat, I heard the odd tones – odd on Athos, where most visitors seem German or Scandinavian – of an American voice.

Wondering what eager middle-aged academic was holding forth, I made my way back to the benches at the stern, only to find an old fellow, with snow-white beard chatting way to some pilgrims in his broad accent. Even as he did so, he went on plaiting one of the small rosaries made out of rope that is a typical gift from monk to pilgrim. Such are the connections which wind and unwind on the slopes of the Holy Mountain. Perhaps when I first passed his hermitage, the train of yuppified backpackers – an express in the Italian sense – had scared him off.

On Athos I was sorry to have only had a glancing encounter with the hermit tradition. This is logical enough yet I wanted to have the chance to explore some of the themes of that life, including the ones which were, paradoxically, so much about the world, and the connection the lone monk has with it. Above all I wanted to talk through the idea of the solitary as a man or woman of action: a heroic figure whose closeness to God, honed through long feats of self-denial and contemplation, prepares him or her for the role of intervening in secular society, on behalf of the marginalized and down-trodden. I felt that such a discussion would have much to teach me, as far as the work I was about to embark on in Britain was concerned. I wanted to draw deep from the fountain while I still had the chance. But it was not to be. I did not feel like disturbing the peaceful conversation then in progress, and this would be the last time I saw this chatty hermit, a Philadelphian to the very core.

Thinking of the best things in the monastic tradition made me determined to find a warmer welcome elsewhere, and so when the time came, I walked out of Xeropotamou without regrets. Since the monastery is closed from morning till early afternoon, the main gates were due to shut in a few minutes. Clearly the host of pilgrims who had materialized out of nowhere for that service, of unhappy experience, had decided to stay for more. Or had they perhaps already fled?

And yet there had been consolations in my visit. First there was the wonderful view from the arbour, which I came upon as I strolled round the monastery grounds on my first evening, and where, later on in my stay, I had a long and pleasant chat with two inter-railers. One of these, a Norwegian, had come equipped with a bottle of gin. The other, an Israeli, fresh from his military service, was keeping his anthropological eyes open, he told me. Certainly the time I spent with them was not one of my typical experiences of Athos. Yet it was good to sit up late into the night, having a true traveller's conversation – where they'd been, how many continents, and all the rest. I'd pretty much given up, in any case, on the monastic front that day, at this least hospitable of convents. My two new friends were, I felt, a godsend of a diversion at this point on my walking tour.

Ten minutes down the path in the morning, our ways split: the two backpackers headed off down the bleak road to Dafni and beyond, the main thoroughfare of Athos. Like most outsiders they only had four-day passes, and so it was crucial they made the boat connection.

My own way was something of a treat by comparison. I was headed for Ayiou Panteleimonos, the Russian monastery, known familiarly in Greek – although with something of a ring of distrust about the word – simply as 'the Roussikon'. Tensions between idiorrythmic and coenobitic communities are only rivalled by those between the various national groupings of Orthodox monks. Pan-Orthodoxy has never been any easier to hold together on Athos than in the world at large.

The path to Panteleimonos now skirted a blunt densely wooded headland, and was a welcome change from the dramatic crags of the south-east. Soft ground and occasional clearings made for a gentle walk with frequent leisurely stops. I took my time along the route.

Panteleimonos itself was an abrupt shock. In the nineteenth century this was a huge place, spreading out along the waterfront like a small town. Although most of the buildings survive in a parlous, ramshackle state, the difference between then and now is the numbers. Literally thousands of Russian monks inhabited the monastery in the nineteenth century, encouraged by their government in a bid for dominance of the Mountain, and the legacy of this aggrandisement has cost the convent dear. Fearful of Russian designs even now – there have been constant rumours over the past few years of KGB machinations – the ruling executive has consistently forbidden the rebuilding of the gutted wings. They stand now like great abandoned hulks in a sea of weeds.

In spite of the continuing offers of money from the Russian government, Greek opposition has had its way. There may have been a few monks here, but there was at the time of my visit no guesthouse of which to speak. And yet there remained something finely elegant about this oasis of Slavic culture with its tapering domes and gaudy colours. As one Orthodox wit put it, the domes are supposed to resemble candle flames, but people always think of onions! I was sorry there was nobody to show me round. Walking away along the beach, I turned once to capture the place on film, and then it was on through the woods to Xenofontos.

Here I spent an uneventful night, in a dormitory with three Greek lads, definitely from the curiosity school of pilgrims. The guesthouse was atmospheric in its plainness – oil-lamps, requiring considerable nous to light, lit the bare walls in fitful flickers. I felt welcome, although strangely I met no guestmaster the whole time I was there. Had he retired sick, I wondered, to be taken off to the infirmary to be fed better rations, as Benedict prescribes? There were two fine things about Xenofontos, however – the spectacular frescoes of the *trapezaria*, and a garden that was quite lovely.

The next morning I was faced with my great choice, the one that would lead, as I was about to discover, either to the Balkans or to the mid-west. It was one of those difficult choices between conscience and ease with which the Athonite pilgrimage, like most travel, is full. The prospect of a lift on the boat is often beguiling but it has, as I have mentioned, its own vicissitudes – the stress of erratic arrangements is sometimes more of an ordeal than the simple exertion of walking. Should I hitch back to Dafni, or press on to Dohiariou, a half-hour or so away? And where from there? What would I have time for? The web of paths that covers the inland monasteries – Kastamonitou, Zografou, Hilandariou, Esfigmenou – does so in hefty distances of three to four hours at a stretch. These monasteries would perhaps have proved the most revealing of my trip, by virtue of the contrast they present, for they include the sole surviving idiorrythmic monastery, the convent of Hilandariou. Not only that, but here too I might get a chance to shed some more light on relations between Athos, Orthodoxy and the world – for Hilandariou, like no other monastery on Athos at this troubled time, was still Serbian.

Every traveller has his or her moment of weakness, a moment when you wonder if the stress of enquiry is really worth it. Bill Bryson, I remembered, had abandoned his search for native culture while on the Appalachian trail. And what about Peter Levi in Afghanistan? In the comforting shadow of the greats, I made my own compromise now, as the intensity of the Mountain threatened, not for the first time, to overwhelm me. International politics, as well as asceticism, was just too much.

So I decided to walk on to Dohiariou, and from there to try and pick up the mid-morning arrival of the pilgrim boat as it made its way on to Dafni. From there I might catch the bus to Karies and even reach the capital in time for lunch. I had only been through its outskirts, on the way to the Lavra in Theoliptos' jeep on my very first day, and so, by this stage, I was eager for my first sight of the famous church of the Protaton, belonging to the ruling council of Athos.

The walk to Dohiariou was the easiest of this stretch along the south-west coast. When I arrived, I was immediately glad of my choice. Dohiariou is a high-walled garden of delights, of ferns and orange-trees, through which a path ascends along a steep row of buildings, monkly domiciles and chapels. Almost a tiny vertical village, it is a truly enchanting place. I pottered around its alleys and courts, all highly condensed, and as I was ordered by a stern sign, resisted the urge to photograph the beautiful frescoed *phiale* at the heart of one of them.

Dohiariou has the merest of harbours, a single concrete jetty projecting from the shingle beach. The walls of the convent were never high enough, and in the absence of natural defences it suffered badly in the Middle Ages. Occasional sorties by the imperial fleet were never enough to deter marauding pirates, although Constantinople did provide some money for repairs. Usually there was just enough time to effect these before the next round of attacks began. I understood now why Christos had shivered – it was a frightening time to be a monk on Mount Athos.

I sat down at the waterfront to read as I waited for the pilgrim-boat. The only perils now were a couple of dour workers and their frisky dog. Although, when it arrived, the boat sailed alarmingly past us, in good time it reversed, lowered its tail-gate and allowed the four of us on board. I joined the eager throng whose first glimpse this was of an Athonite monastery, as it must be their first of a foot-sore pilgrim. Your turn will come, I chuckled to myself as I sank down next to a post-bag.

CHAPTER 6

Karies

Since my first arrival on Athos, I had felt the influence that spread out from the capital, Karies. Here was the majesty of power forgotten in our advanced democracies – authority unimpeachable and unapproachable. The Protaton, the Epistasia, the Protos – First Lord of Athos – himself, these are not the quaint survivals of a bygone realpolitik. When I needed to have my *diamonitirion* extended, it was brought here by the Lavra's representative to the Holy Council, the administrative executive of Athos. Policing the thousands of pilgrims at the height of summer is a serious business, and is enforced as such. I was dependent on the Protaton every day of my sojourn.

It was the beautiful Church of the Protaton in the main square of Karies I had mainly come to see. By the time the pilgrim bus lumbered into action, hauling itself up the same hilly route that Theoliptos in the AO15 jeep had managed to scramble over with the rest of us that very first day, I arrived to find the church was shut for mid-day, a time of general inaction throughout Greece. The forbidding doors were definitely very firmly sealed. Since there was nobody in sight to ask, I took my place on the steps opposite alongside a stray dog and prepared to enjoy what everyone else was no doubt enjoying, a brief siesta out of the battling sun.

Karies is a very strange place, perhaps even stranger than

the rest of the Mountain. Elsewhere things bustle quietly on in a familiar way. Here in the capital, however, live those who, not having a monastic vocation themselves, are charged with providing services for the rest of the peninsula. There is, for example, a post office, where I stopped to post a letter. It maintains the sole telephone link with the mainland that is available to outsiders. There are others in individual monasteries and in fact a network of shaky wires is strung along the entire length of the coast. As I thought of jackals, on my long and lonely walks, often these wires were something tangibly worldly to focus on. Somehow the hum of telecommunications, however ancient they might be, left me feeling a little less alone.

Also at Karies there are the headquarters of the Athonite police, who form part of the Greek national constabulary. The monks themselves who live here are either engaged in the official administration at the Protaton, or involved in the minor tourist industry sustained by the constant flow of pilgrims. Since both of Athos' main ports – Iviron on the north coast, Dafni on the south – are served by the remarkable bus service, pilgrims flow in daily, to buy souvenirs along Karies' main street. This stretches from the main square, at one end, where the church is found, to the bus-stop at the other. Along its length, riders – monastic or otherwise – are required to dismount. Pilgrims graze the row of gift shops selling popular icons and Athos memorabilia. Halfway down the street is the sole restaurant of the capital – the one at Dafni is the only other – and many are the desperate pilgrims who have succumbed to its otherworldly 'temptations'.

Apart from the boutique monks, who often seem to be the hoariest – perhaps for reasons of the picturesque – a small number of others live on the outskirts of the town in individual *kalyvai,* working on the land or in their craft studios. Finally, there is the school, now I believe, defunct, which used to supply the monasteries with a steady stream of recruits. By taking boys at a young age, rather like the Janissary corps of the Ottomans, the school could instil the Athonite ethos in those who would never know another way of life. Nowadays, most new monks of Athos come to their vocation after early adulthood.

As I sat outside the police HQ, with my mangy companion – some monk's best friend, perhaps – I found myself thinking back to my previous experience with this crack detachment of law enforcers. It was not my first encounter with what is an understandably but, nevertheless, spectacularly uneager outfit. When I awoke on my very first morning at the Lavra – it seemed a long time ago by now – I remembered I had left my money-belt on the back of a toilet door, just outside the *archondariki.*

'Here you do not need money' had been the advice of Theoliptos, way back in the April before my arrival. Nevertheless I had brought some 20,000 drachmas from the mainland – about £40 at that time – in case of emergency. Where I was intending to spend it, I am not now sure, since Athos is not a place you can grab a taxi by flourishing wads of cash.

By the time I returned to the loo, I was dismayed to find all my drachmas had disappeared. Strangely the purse remained – a thoughtful touch – to hang forlornly on the peg where I had left it the day before. Indeed everything else in it had survived, from credit cards to travellers' cheques. It was a humbling moment. Where else would a thief – who in this case had probably to do quite a few days' work for this kind of money – have missed the opportunity to disguise his work and abandon all the evidence, if he had no further use for it?

When Theoliptos rang me on the internal phone, I relayed the entire sorry tale and he hurried over to discuss the matter. There are many people milling around an Athos monastery at this time of year. In addition to the monastic community proper, there are the pilgrims, the devout and the curious, and the large numbers of lay brothers who come for the summer in return for free board and lodging. It could have been anyone – a passing visitor, or, far more disturbingly, one of the familiar faces whom I found myself watching suspiciously over lunch in the trapezaria from then on.

Yet help was at hand. Theoliptos rang the police in Karies and one of their number duly arrived in his jeep, his *Hellenike astinomia* shirt hanging loosely out of a pair of grimy jeans. I played my part of Watson with studious vigour, as Jeans-man took me back to the scene of the crime. There we proceeded to a meticulous examination of the evidence. As we squeezed into the cubicle, I pointed out the very peg where the calumny had occurred. Jeans-man nodded wisely. We squeezed out again and returned to the *archondariki*. The only thing missing, to add to the comedy, was a Cluedo-like secret passage.

I already knew we would never arraign our miscreant but Jeans-man pointed emphatically down at the guest ledger, as if discovering proof for the first time. 'Look,' he said, 'many people . . .' and then, 'they have gone.' It was, I nodded gravely, incontrovertible. A group of so-called 'pilgrims' had checked out that morning! By now they would be well on their way with the lolly.

Sitting in Karies beside my faithful Cerberus, I could see

the recalcitrant members of what I began to call the West Athos Serious Crime Squad, as they sat around undoubtedly planning their next boar hunt. Their high jinks spilled out, from time to time, onto the balcony of their HQ, alongside which a ragged Greek flag hung limply on its pole. How bored they must be.

*

In Karies, I was no longer Matthaios but Mathieu. 'Tu as le nom de l'évangeliste,' remarked my new friend, not entirely originally. It did not much matter since Moise Filogenou was larger than life. Later, I would sit with him in the cafés and restaurants of Thessalonika – an experience that was strangely, even intensely, relaxing after being on Mount Athos. From our bizarre conversations – the engagement of my halting French with a lilting Creole patois – I was to learn the most about Orthodox spirituality, Kallistos Ware and others not withstanding. Moise must rank as a strange breed – an Orthodox pilgrim from Guadeloupe – but as he eulogized everything from the wonders of his faith to the weather 'à Carribe', I listened spellbound. We ranged over the whole terrain, from married priests to the unfortunate Latin sack of Constantinople. Over our plate of kalamari in the single taverna of the capital, he sang out his view of the gospel – one of *l'amour,* to which East–West differences, indeed all human oppositions, must ultimately bow. Moise's own brother, recently married, is a Catholic. Was there a tension there for him? 'C'est la même chose, la même église.'

In Guadeloupe, I learnt, a place is still set for 'l'ange qui passe'. Now, Moise picked up the bill (the globe-trotting resources of this icon-painter were a mystery). Before he sent me on my way, he bound up a package in front of me – a gift of some tiny laminated icons for a Greek family who ran a restaurant in London. A man like Moise does not make friends in the ordinary way, so much as pull you half-miraculously into his world. I was to see it done to others in due course. 'Mathieu,' he called out after me as he shouldered his bag, 'tu as ta commission.'

I would meet Moise again, and yet he was already, from our first meeting, a vitally important connection for me between the world of Athos and the one beyond. Here was a pilgrim I could discuss and even argue with, while all the time keeping in view the dense spirituality of the Holy Mountain. Because he was vibrant in his Orthodox faith, yet open to understanding and alliances between different versions of the Christian story, and because I could communicate with him well enough in a shared tongue, I felt that he really was in some sense my own passing Athonite angel.

Later when we got back to the mainland, it seemed as if we had brought a piece of the Holy Mountain's rarefied peace back along with us. It was impossible to sit in a pavement café and not think of where we had journeyed together. Had I come back completely alone, I am sure the waters of normality would have closed over my head much faster. As it was, here was one last chance to breathe two airs simultaneously, to smell the flowers of the Mountain one last time, before the exhaust-fumes of Thessalonika blocked them out for ever.

After our lunch, I emerged a little giddily from the inn – had that really been a litre of Greek-brewed Amstel? – and stumbled into the oven-like heat that rises from the ground during the early afternoon. Setting off through the outskirts of Karies, I hoped to find a bed at the monastery of Koutloumoussiou. This place did not come well recommended. As I mentioned to the two Brits Ian and

David, when we reconnected later, my guidebook had pronounced the condemnation that 'by far the most interesting thing about the place' was its name, which is believed to be that of a Moslem convert.

After my one single experience of the place, I cannot say much interest besides this ever developed for me. Ascetic considerations aside, there was little reason for me not to give the place the benefit of the doubt, until, that is, the strange reception I received there. No longer would I be much disposed to offer Koutloumousiou my charity. Equally dishevelled, the convent proved even less welcoming than Xeropotamou. 'No, I could not stay,' announced the door keeper without explanation.

Certainly the place was busy with renovations; but it would surely have been reasonable to expect some refreshment nonetheless, even if nothing more than a glass of water. In many places – the monastery of Iviron for one – I was to get far kinder treatment in almost identical circumstances. A place that was too busy, or possibly otherwise engaged, would still try to do all it could to refresh the passing pilgrim. It was not, however, as I reflected, a disaster. With what I thought was the sure prospect of finding somewhere to stay in this sprawling place, I headed back to the centre of Karies.

In the end, this was not to be. My second bet was the skete of St Andrew, whose grandiose architecture with an array of green domes, bespoke its origin as a dependency of the Roussikon. I could not fully appreciate this at the time, being denied entry here as well. How many monasteries had to be undergoing restoration, just when I needed to stay in them? Now my picture of the place is the lovely one engraved on my memory: orange trees, and a grandeur that had faded into a certain ascetic gentility. Unlike the Russian itself, this place had not gone to wrack and ruin. In the garden, a lone monk rested in the crook of a tree, striking what I took to be a classic Athonite pose in his meditations. The huge difference between us, occurred to me now – he with his thoughts, me with my temporal agenda, seeking only somewhere to lay my head. Left standing outside yet another guesthouse, it was all I could do to maintain an outward show of decorum and tranquillity. All such feelings had fled by this time in my search for the hospitality to which I believed myself entitled. The heat too had left me on a short fuse.

In the end I gave up waiting and returned to the mean hostel that passed as a pilgrim hotel, in a side-street off the main square. Resigning myself to the most depressing conditions yet, I lay down in my meagre, dirty room for a late siesta, my second of the afternoon. It was proving to be a long one.

I awoke after an hour to answer once again the call of the Spirit – whether human or divine, I am not quite sure. I could not possibly spend the night here, it told me, not in these conditions, when I hardly needed to, with that *diamonitirion* in my hand. So, on a sudden inspiration, I exchanged some curt words with the card-playing staff and struck out for the cluster of monasteries on the north coast. Exhilarated despite my exhaustion, I did not even know exactly where I was heading. For once, perhaps for the first real time, I was trusting in something higher.

The road led quickly into dense scrub. Still hoping for shelter at a local *skiti* or *kalyve,* I turned off onto a track, which led towards some isolated buildings. The first lot were deserted, but at the second, I found signs of habitation: a pile of walking sticks leant against the outer door of a tumble-down shack. I knocked loudly, but getting no answer, struggled on through the brambles which guarded a path into the wood engulfing the place.

Only when I emerged into a clearing did I realize I was being hailed. The voice from behind was that of a hermit who lived at the shack. He was waving vigorously for me to wend my way back through the wood. Once I had returned, he offered me some water, muttering it over and over again in Greek – 'nero, nero, nero' – and even supplied me with one of the sticks from the pile outside his door that was ready for just such an occasion. Nodding with satisfaction as he tried it for strength, he handed it over and pointed me in the direction of the main road. Ian and David would later confirm they had met this kindly hermit, just as I, it seemed, had met theirs.

The scenery along the track was now unlike any I had yet come across. Rolling plains were covered by a low carpet of shrubs, rising up to the slopes of Mount Athos itself in the distance. I could see for miles ahead, as I made my way down into the valley beyond the town. This was the wide open, uninhabited countryside I had seen in my imagination before coming here, and it was quite simply a delight. Most of the paths I had trodden wound their way round the outer slopes of the peninsula, with the sea on one side and dense forest, or sheer rock, on the other. On most there was no landward view at all. Monasteries would come leaping out of a cliff-face when you were almost beneath them, just as Edward Lear was taken by surprise at every corner by the views that he stopped to paint so stunningly.

Now I caught sight of the next monastery, Iviron, when it was still several miles and a couple of hours' walking in the distance. The road, I knew, would fork eventually, one prong leading there while the other branched off to the convent of Stavronikita. At the end of this long day of disasters I did not feel as if I should risk another one. On the notice-board at the Ouranopoli Pilgrim Bureau, there had been a sign warning potential guests to book places at Iviron a day in advance. I took the other road.

The convent of Stavronikita, named for the 'victory of the cross', looked recently restored when I reached it, the stone a golden colour just like Oxford's after its cleaning in recent years. From afar it shone in the afternoon sun. The huge blunt crenellations looked like a parody of fortification, but were quite possibly intended as such, even as they towered over a beautiful garden. Through this, the approach led me to the main gate where the monks had had the bright idea of constructing a tiny welcoming room, just outside the portal itself – a testament to the present redundancy of the hefty walls. This little cabin doubled as a breakfast-room and, were it not for the lateness of my arrival, I would have been treated to coffee and ouzo here as well. The leftovers of the previous fortunate arrivals were still waiting to be washed up when I introduced myself to the *archondaris*. It was almost time for the pilgrim supper which was eaten separately from the community, no matter what one's faith. At least, for once, I was included in the exclusion!

I shared a room with a young Greek guy from Athens, who woke me in the morning to see the spectacular sunrise, a real rosy-fingered dawn, from the living-room of the *archondarikion*. Projecting from the outer wall on a timber balcony, the guesthouse here was one of those perilous Athonite creations that makes you feel, as one academic observed recently, considerably closer to God than you might do elsewhere. The room had fantastic views out to sea and along the coast in each direction, to the monastery of Pantocrators in the west, and in the east, to Iviron. The sun came up in moments, rushing over the horizon and slowing as it climbed. And so, majestically, I had come to the penultimate day of my tour.

CHAPTER 7

. . . and back to the Lavra

The last two days of walking were to be the longest, and the first began with a mission. In fairness to Ian and David, the flagging Brits, I owe them an acknowledgment for the piece of advice that was the most useful, and perhaps the most humbling for me, on this final stretch of my journey. According to a Greek friend of theirs, it was customary to present the guestmaster of a monastery with a small gift, upon one's departure. The fact that I never saw this done by any other pilgrim, Greek or non-Greek, did not lessen my estimation of this idea. Moreover, once I had learned of it, I reckoned it only reasonable, after his months of trouble on my account, that I should remember my own host in just such a way. Accordingly, I decided to leave Stavronikita that morning, and return to Karies. Much as I disliked the commercial aspect of that place, first time round, I was glad it would now be useful in the fulfilment of my debt.

I found out, that if I walked a mile or so out of the monastery gates, I would be able to connect with the bus that came from Iviron. The way led back up to the fork where, the night before, I had made my fortuitous, and certainly inspired, decision to turn off towards the wonderful monastery of Stavronikita. It was a happy walk and once there I spent a good twenty minutes eavesdropping on a theological discussion conducted in English between an open-minded

Protestant ordinand and a couple of Greeks. It ranged over
the whole spectrum of Orthodox beliefs and practices, most
of which I had recently been reading about in a variety of
books gleaned from the guesthouses of the Mountain. It was
almost as if they had taken their list of topics for discussion
from the same. The group broke off their discussion
momentarily to take a picture of me, but the rest were true
to Gregory of Nyssa's caricature of life in Constantinople:

> The whole city is full of it, the squares, the market-
> places, the cross-roads, the alleyways; old-clothes
> men, money changers, food sellers: they are all busy
> arguing. If you ask someone to give you change,
> he philosophizes about the Begotten and the
> Unbegotten; if you inquire about the price of a loaf,
> you are told by way of reply that the Father is greater
> and the Son inferior; if you ask 'Is my bath ready?' the
> attendant answers that the Son was made out of
> nothing.
>
> *On the Deity of the Son*, trans. Kallistos Ware

It was a shame the bus arrived to interrupt all their talk, but I
enjoyed the scenery once again – with rather more leisure
this time – as the bus *sauntered* along the road back to the
capital. How wrong the surly guys at that sad hotel had been
when they challenged my decision to stumble on last night,
trusting I would find a proper welcome somewhere on the
Mountain. 'No good go to Iviron' indeed!

We reached the town in what seemed like no time at all,
despite the pace of the Athonite public transport to which
we sore-footed band of pilgrims had rashly entrusted our
lives. Admittedly the bus broke down several hundred yards

out of the capital, but we had made it safely enough, and so I headed for the main street where I was able, somewhat bizarrely, to secure a bottle of scotch for Theoliptos and his *archondarikion* at a very fair price. It was only then, with my priorities in order, and after quite some sojourn, that I finally had my opportunity to see the glorious Church of the Protaton.

Karies remained, on second impressions, a distinctly odd town, a place that seemed as if it had been bound into a straitjacket of commercial and administrative importance, considerably against the grain of its own nature, not to mention the preferences of everybody there, whether clerical, monastic or lay. Because of its importance, I was able to take advantage – or perhaps to be taken advantage of – and restock on exorbitantly priced film as well as other necessities, or rather some unnecessaries, of travel. It was then, as I wandered out into the main square, that I bumped into Ian and David once again, the very pair whose good advice it had been to make my diversion to the north of the peninsula.

Athos, like anywhere else where people walk at their own pace, to connect and reconnect and tell the stories of their experiences, is the perfect place to share the simple human moment of giving such advice. Ian and David had got it right again, as they had before with the Philadelphian hermit. What was it Paul said about human wisdom? Now, six years later, I wonder what they think of Mount Athos. That they remember it well, I have no doubts. Some people tell their stories of places like Athos in sudden relief at their return, while others leave them to simmer for a season. Still others find that the story becomes their whole life. For the present, Ian and David were quitting the Mountain, worn out by heat and the alien culture of the place, or perhaps they had just been floored by a surfeit of religion. In fact it was not so much Orthodoxy, I suspected, that had got to them, as the sudden untrammelled deluge of spirituality that is an unavoidable part of the experience of being on the Mountain. It is a thing from which there is little relief – except in occasional encounters with other pilgrims. Had there not been enough of these for Ian and David, perhaps?

So I bid them farewell and good luck. I was not even sure they would make it as far as the boat, and got to wondering if this is how people find themselves converted to the monastic life of Athos. Do they simply run out of steam – the energy it takes to leave a place as bewilderingly, frustratingly, magnetic as it is? In the end, I trusted that something, some spirit of rightness about these things, would protect them – since, I am sure, it was not for them – and went off to make, at last, my visit to the church.

*

It was well worth the wait. The spacious beauty of the nave, with its marvellous frescoes, befitted the importance of this place in the Athonite order of things. The monk who showed me round smiled when I told him I was from Oxford. There are certainly enough academics who visit Athos out of professional interest, combined with more than a little plain and simple curiosity. In recent months, the distinguished Byzantinist Sir Stephen Runciman had been before me to the Lavra, to be served watermelon by Theoliptos, I have no doubt! I thanked my guide and repaired to the taverna, unfortunately this time without Moise, to plan what would be the last leg of my journey.

My final two experiences of Athonite monasteries, as I made my way back to my own erstwhile home on the

Mountain, could not have been more different from each other. In Karies, I managed to catch the pilgrim-bus bound for Iviron – it seemed I was to get there after all – and got on with a straggle of pilgrims. Just before, I had a satisfying exchange with another pilgrim, in which I used all four of my picked-up phrases. Mistaking these for fluency in the language, the demure gentleman I had quizzed about the bus came to my rescue with a quick translation of his own answer.

Stepping off the bus at Iviron some minutes later, I found my young Greek friends from Xenofontos sitting in a disconsolate huddle by the wharf. 'You cannot stay here', they warned, and so it seemed the signs I had encountered, back along the way, were not wrong. Nor had the boat from Ierissos been along this northern coast for several days. I seemed, therefore, to be faced with a fair walk to one of the nearest monasteries – inland to Filotheou or on to Karakallou. I couldn't return to Stavronikita, however much I might prefer it, since one night at each place is the *diamonitirion* rule.

Still I was determined to try my luck here at Iviron and so, leaving my friends at the *arsanas*, I climbed the gentle slope to the monastery gate. The group of Greek pilgrims ahead of me quickly vanished into the woodwork, having presumably booked in advance for the upcoming feast. A monk approached as I stood alone at the door, but from his gesticulations I surmised I was not to be in luck. An English-speaking monk stepped in to help. No, I couldn't stay, but if I wished, I might have some water. I gladly took him up on the offer and so was passed on to a third monk, this time an Australian, who patiently led me over to the pump. A Laurel and Hardy-like scene ensued in which we struggled with the thing, unable to make it work. Suddenly a group of work-men emerged from the ground and began signalling at us apologetically. Seconds later the water gushed afresh.

Iviron, my host explained, was due to host a festival to which about a thousand pilgrims were coming. The whole place was being intensively cleaned and repaired. I could, however, look round the church. Indeed I was given a guided tour with a parallel Greek translation for a second non-Anglophone pilgrim. Preparations in the church were hectic, but it was one of the richest sights I had seen. Inside, Iviron boasts one of the marvels of Athos, the miracle-work-ing icon, the Portaitissa. To let me see this treasure, the 'Virgin Guarding the Gate', was a great favour in the circumstances, and one that I very much appreciated. For the whole of my trip I had been unable to gain entry to the libraries and treasure-stores of the monasteries I had visited. After the pilferings of Robert Curzon and others, the monks are careful when they make exceptions to their rules in such matters. The Virgin in the icon has a beautiful veil in a relief of beaten silver, encircling the painted face of the Panagia, Protectress of Athos, which has become darkened over the years. Legend has it that disaster will befall the Mountain should the icon ever leave. A row of watches and trinkets lines the case which covers her. The former impressed me greatly – placed here by thankful devotees, they are a fitting symbol for life on Athos, the abandonment of time to the divine.

My Australian host, unlike many monks quite a shy man, was generous of his own time amidst the construction, and talked to me briefly about spirituality. At the end of our con-versation he found me a copy of a pamphlet published by his brother back in Australia, and gave me an extra one for the *archondariki* back at the Lavra. Theoliptos, it turned out, would be most unimpressed, displaying – for monastic reasons, as I supposed – a complete lack of interest in the same. I felt it would take me a stay of several months to fathom this kind of detachment, especially when it concerned the very things which are supposed to make monastic life tick. Perhaps one needs to practise to understand.

Nevertheless I had been heartened, after my few recent bad experiences among all the many better ones, by all this care and concern at Iviron. Despite the continuing fruitlessness of my second day spent searching for a bed, I set out in a good mood on the coastal road once more, bound this time, I had decided, for Karakallou. The walk went up and down a boring sandy road, as the fine view of Iviron's harbour and the coastal line of convents from which I had come – Stavronikita standing out proud in the distance – were almost immediately eclipsed by trees on all sides. This was the very same forest I had been spooked by on my first day, as I crouched in the bank of Theoliptos' monk-mobile. Now, although I was no longer frightened, the way became very long and wearying.

Eventually rescue came, in the form of a huge transporter lorry. The monk was direct in his speech, though not unfriendly, and at the end of a ride that was occasionally hair-raising – I expected it by now – he dropped me off at the end of the long walkway leading up through the wood to my destination. I struggled up a vicious incline for half an hour and finally made it to the gates of Karakallou. On the last night of my tour, I was to receive my very worst welcome yet. Though afforded the regular sustenance on arrival, the *archondaris* was surly in the extreme, and arrangements at supper later were little better. After church, from which I was excluded, I sat in the courtyard with numerous cats and their fleas. After the communal meal had been concluded in the *trapezaria*, I entered to make my own lonely repast. No one, save my two room-mates, ever spoke to me, and that was only to assault me with the kind of fierce views which are typically espoused by those who live at a safe distance from ethnic problems. They were two aggressive Australians who spent the evening polemicizing me on the Macedonian Question.

The last stretch of my tour was a gruelling four-hour walk. It led along the ten miles of bleak coastal road to the Lavra, the same stretch whose ecological implications I had mulled over, while sitting on the wheel of Theoliptos' jeep. In fact I had taken a gamble after breakfast at Karakallou, and waited a good hour into the morning to see if the boat was coming. Since this is the stormy north coast, it did not do so and thus, by the time I quit the monastery, scene of a very dismal sojourn, it was already 10 o'clock. The air was heating up at a worrying rate.

By noon I had made it to the saw-mill where previously I had seen the illicit bathing-practices of a hoary *kalyve*-dweller. The interconnections of the Holy Mountain went on, and so now it was his partner who kindly gave me water before sending me on my way. Beyond this outpost, there remained, I reckoned, a further six good miles. I saw nobody at all the whole time, and pressed on towards the *eremos*, the wilderness at the southern tip of Athos, on whose edge the Lavra itself lies.

In the ascetic tradition, it is in the deepest desert the heart finds its freedom. It was this desert that I was rapidly approaching, not as at first in the unascetic luxury of a four-wheel drive, but now on foot, tired, hot, at times disquieted, at times at peace. My walk was turning out to be somewhat like the journey of the monastic life itself.

There were times when I longed for another jeep to roar up behind me. At one point a chopper flew past, bearing what illustrious royals or eminent musicians I could not know. No chance of a lift, but even so I waved. I didn't mind, since this was the first real piece of solitude I had had for a couple of days, and I relished the chance to journey as a true pilgrim for once. Perhaps it was for the very last time.

When very nearly home I drank with glee from the spring-cum-shrine I had visited on my very first day with Theoliptos. Then I upped my pack, loaded with his whisky, and set off on the very last leg, an exhausting hour's yomp. By the end of it, I was ready to give up and lie down with the wolves. Just then the very next clearing brought elation, revealing the broad west wall of my home, missed through the long days of my journey round the Mountain. Once more I was back at the monastery of *Megiste Lavra*, the Grand Lavra itself. Rushing up to the nearest hillock I snapped a triumphal photograph before dashing down the fifty yards between me and bliss.

Leaping up the steps of the *archondariki* – very unmonastically, three at a time – I sank onto the hard wooden bench as if it were a sultan's divan. A new *dochimos* I had not met came to stand over me. What did I want? In vain I tried to find the words, as he thumbed perplexedly for my name in the Lavra's guestbook. Soon enough Christos put in a timely appearance and slamming the book shut, clapped his hand on our companion's shoulder. Coffee, *loukoumi* and *ouzo* all round!

Epilogue

The boat returning from Athos is a strange place to be. Caught between two worlds, I was far from sure which one I wanted to be in. Stranger still, I sensed that those around me felt the same. About our legs, the bright hues of modern hiking gear pressed us all together, monks and pilgrims. Bad tempers might well have been fuelled by such conditions, and yet despite the fact there was hardly any room in which to move, the mood was subdued, not restless. Perhaps it was the ordeal we had just been through.

Some minutes before, the arduous customs-check, mandatory for all taking leave of the Holy Mountain, had been accomplished with dubious thoroughness and a maximum of fuss. It was no longer irritation, at the antics of the harbour staff, that kept us down now, as we sat bobbing in our boat; yet somehow the normal laughter and wonder of travel, things that ought to be bubbling to the surface on a trip as spectacular as this, had been suppressed. Our high spirits had flown elsewhere, even as the landscape was oblivious, and the lovely coastline unfurled alongside us for the very last time. We breathed in its delights, natural and man-made, almost in silence.

Many of us, as casual nods and glances betrayed, already knew each other. There were several Greek priests returning to the mainland, as well as a smattering of monks, including, curiously enough, Theoliptos, who had maintained a studied, though not antagonistic, silence through the journey of several hours to the port. He was going on monastery business to the mainland – the real world, I remembered now as I looked at the thick black robes about his knees. In an hour or so, we would pile off the boat and the majority of us would slip away into the anonymity of tourism, leaping onto buses, losing ourselves among the postcard shops selling images of the places which for a strange while had been our home.

Not so Theoliptos. For him it would be different – no casual anonymity, as he struggled with bus connections, a little out of practice, perhaps even nervous. Would people be more or less patient with him on account of his dress? How many roadside disputes would he be called on to adjudicate? Would he find what he was looking for in Thessalonika and return home with an easy mind, or would the sights and spirit of the city disturb him, making him wonder why he had ever left to set sail for what remained of a lost Byzantium?

I turned these things over in my mind, and then fell to concentrating on the quick-fire conversation going on in French between my young Greek friends, and my sometime companion Moise Filogenou. They were discussing theology, and culture – the conversation hotting up as we neared land. It was an international crowd, the kind of company in which the insights are fascinating, above all when barely intended, and where you have to keep your wits about you not to offend.

Once off the boat, we soon found our bus and in a matter of no time were chugging along the mountain road back to civilization. Now for the first time, I was suddenly glad to be going home – home, above all, to the world. Theoliptos himself looked more serious than ever, perhaps concentrating against that world, while at the back of the bus, the rest of us kept up our banter – making plans to see each other, to spend time together in the city. There was talk of meals and cheap hotels, and I slipped, without noticing it, into the easy mode of the inter-railing backpacker.

But Athos itself had not left us. Back in Thessalonika, roaming the ways of a once great city, I stumbled over her present-day religion, tiny churches tucked into corners, only noticed by the old men who doffed their hats while passing by. In such places I remembered, from my time on Athos, a sense of having been somewhere where all that trying near to be God had come into the sharpest focus. On the Holy Mountain, where there was no other reason to be there than to pray and to be at peace with others, all the constraints of religion in everyday life – the lack of time, the occasional embarrassment, the feeling that you should be doing something else – simply vanished. There was no other place to go, nor any reason for being there if there were.

I met up with Moise again, and with the others, and we talked about many things, most of them entirely normal. Nevertheless I am sure I was not alone in feeling ever so slightly out of place, somehow apart from all this life. Even the people we saw going about their business now seemed different, and sitting alongside them in cafés made us feel we were thinking of things of which they themselves could have no idea. It was not a feeling of superiority, but it was a sense of difference – difference by experience, not by nature. It was what we had done, not who we were that caused the divide. Something like it I imagine military veterans to feel as they try to ease back into normal life. And yet is a difference that, as Thomas Merton saw, the world may truly need.

Physical solitude has its dangers, but we must not exaggerate them. The great temptation of modern man is not physical solitude but immersion in the mass of other men, not escape to the mountains or the desert. There is actually no more dangerous solitude than that of the man who is lost in a crowd, who does not know he is alone and who does not function as a person in a community either. He does not face the risks of true solitude or its responsibility, and at the same time the multitude has taken all other responsibilities off his shoulders. Yet he is by no means free of care; he is burdened by the diffuse, anonymous anxiety, the nameless fears, the petty itching lusts and all-pervading hostilities which fill mass society the way water fills the ocean.

I am not sure if I shall ever return to Athos, but that feeling, not quite of shellshock, but of a strange awakening, an awakening available to us all, whether we find it, whether we are allowed to find it on Athos or not, it is this my time on the Mountain gave me, even without my expecting or desiring it. There were many of us who came to, and then left, the Mountain through those weeks, just as many monks no doubt also have come and gone. What all of us had in common, what all of us, and many others, must in some way still share, is the experience of having come away again, just that bit changed, just that bit less sure of where true holiness is to be found in our world.

Further Reading

Athos

Bryer, A. and Cunningham, M., 1996, *Mount Athos and Byzantine Monasticism*, Aldershot, Variorum.

Byron, R., 1949, *The Station. Athos: Treasures and Men*, London, John Lehmann.

Constantine, C., 1991, *Anchored in God: Life, Art and Thought on the Holy Mountain of Athos*, Belmont, MA, Institute of Byzantine and Modern Greek Studies.

Dawkins, R.M., 1936, *The Monks of Athos*, London, George Allen & Unwin.

Byzantium

Baynes, N., 1925, *The Byzantine Empire*, London, William Norgate.

Mango, C., 1980, *Byzantium: The Empire of the New Rome*, London, Weidenfeld & Nicolson.

Norwich, J.J., 1998, *A Short History of Byzantium*, London, Penguin.

Early Monasticism

Brown, P., 1989, *The Body and Society: Men, Women and Sexual Renunciation in Early Christianity*, London, Faber and Faber.

Chitty, D., 1977, *The Desert a City*, New York, St Vladimir's Seminary Press.

Gregg, R.C., 1980, *Athanasius: The Life of Antony and the Letter to Marcellinus*, New York.

Ward SLG, B., 1975, *The Sayings of the Desert Fathers*, London, Mowbrays.

Orthodoxy

Ware, K., 1993, *The Orthodox Church*, London, Penguin.

Art

Talbot Rice, D., 1935, *Byzantine Art*, Harmondsworth, Clarendon Press.

Philosophical

Foucault, M., 1985, *The Use of Pleasure* (*The History of Sexuality* Vol. 2), New York, Random House.

Merton, T., 1977, *Raids on the Unspeakable*, Tunbridge Wells, Burns & Oates.

Merton, T., 1972, *Seeds of Contemplation*, Wheathampstead, Anthony Clarke Books.

Merton, T., 1948, *The Seven Storey Mountain*, New York, Harcourt, Brace & Co.

General

Cary-Elwes, C., 1992, *Work & Prayer. The Rule of St Benedict for Lay People*, Tunbridge Wells, Burns & Oates.

Norris, K., 1996, *The Cloister Walk*, New York, Putnam Publishing Group.

Tinsley, A., 1995, *Pax: the Benedictine Way*, Dublin, Columba Press.

Whiteaker, S., 1998, *The Good Retreat Guide*, London, Rider.

Glossary

Accidie: A famous problem in monastic life: the feeling of spiritual boredom or distemper that overtakes the monk once he has successfully learned the first stages of contemplation.

Agion Oros: Holy Mountain, the second name for Mount Athos in Greek.

Archondarikion, colloq. *Archondariki*: Guesthouse, guest-quarters. The colloquial version is truncated from the 'pure' dialect form (see *Katharevoussa*).

Archondaris: Guestmaster.

Arsanas: Harbour, often fortified.

Askesis: Literally training or exercise, the Greek word came to be associated with spiritual endeavour, and has now lost its original athletic connotations.

Astinomia: One of the branches of the Greek police who have headquarters on Athos.

Bouleuterion: Council chamber (ancient).

Chalkidike: The three-fingered peninsula of which Mount Athos is the easternmost promontory. It can be spelt a number of ways in English. The main problem with all systems of transliteration is that, as T.E. Lawrence put it, they are only of help to those who do not need helping. Consistency in rendering Greek words and names always ends in bizarre combinations and so I have not struggled to achieve it here.

Coenobion – *coenobium* hence *coenobite, coenobitic*: *Coenobion* (better than *Koinobion*) is the Greek form, *coenobium* the Latin. The term refers literally to 'the common life', and as a result to the monastery in which this is lived. A coenobite is a monk resident there, and the adjective '*coenobitic*' describes things to do with the monastic arrangements and life in such a place.

Diamonitirion: The four-day monastery pass released to all visitors to the Holy Mountain, and which can on rare occasions be extended for non-Orthodox travellers.

Dochimos: Novice.

Epistasia: The four-man executive of the ruling council (see *Protaton*).

Evangelical counsels, counsels of perfection: Christ's injunction to his followers to sell all they have and follow him; generally taken as the manifesto of Christian asceticism.

Gerondas: Holy man or elder (compare Russian *staretz*); often after years in community, the elder would seek the higher path of spiritual solitude. In many cases, as with Dostoyevsky's famous Father Zosima, the elder would continue to receive visitors to pass on the fruits of his wisdom to them, and help them in times of need.

Iconodule: A supporter of the pro-icon party in any of the various disputes in the history of Orthodoxy, concerning the appropriateness of icons. The opponents of the iconodules were the iconoclasts.

Iconostasis: A stand, or sometimes a screen, in a Greek or other Orthodox church which holds one or more icons for the faithful to venerate.

Kaiki: Ferry, small craft.

Kajmakam: Literally headman, or overseer. William Dalrymple, in *From the Holy Mountain*, also came across this legacy of the Ottoman empire.

Kalli mera: Good day.

Kalyve, pl. kalyvai: A monastic dwelling housing two or more – but no more than a few – monks.

Katharevoussa: The 'pure' dialect held in veneration by certain institutions and groups in Greece, including the Church. Newspapers are sometimes written in it, but the look or sound of it can seem forced in every-day Greek conversation. Signs and speech in Athos range across the divide.

Katholikon: The largest, principal, church of a monastery.

Kellion, pl. kellia: A monastic cell, accommodating a single monk in most cases.

Kiriakon: The principal church of a skete. In idiorrhythmic communities, worship is held here once a week, on Sundays.

Lavra: Literally 'way' or 'path'; comes to refer to an association of monastic cells in a particular area, where the monks loosely share their prayer life with each other.

Leitourgia: The Greek name for the Mass.

Loukoumi: Turkish delight, although it is never called this in Greece.

Ouzo, Raki, Metaxa: Three brands of an alcoholic aniseed drink akin to Ricard or Pernod.

Panagia: All holy. Epithet of Mary, Mother of God.

Phiale: A large fort, often outside the main church of a monastery.

Protaton: The ruling council of Athos.

Skiti, pl. skitai: (English: skete) A village-like community, not necessarily idiorrhythmic – there are coenobitic sketes as well.

Staretz: See *Gerondas*.

Telonia: The toll-houses staffed by demons through which the pious soul must pass on its way to heaven.

Trapezaria: Refectory, dining hall of a monastery.

Typikon: The founding charter of a monastery. Several beautiful Byzantine examples survive.